'09

De...
Thank You for being my friend
May we move into the next years
and become closer and more
creative and productive.
With love —
Beth (Ames Swartz)

The Word in Paint

The Word in Paint
绘画中的哲学

Paintings by

BETH AMES SWARTZ

Inspired by the Poetry of

杜甫 (DU FU, 712–770 A.C.E., Chinese)
李白 (LI BAI, 701–762 A.C.E., Chinese)

Contemporary Poetic Responses to the Swartz Paintings by

BECKIAN FRITZ GOLDBERG

ILIANA ROCHA   LEAH SODERBERG   JOHN SPARROW

Essays by

DONALD KUSPIT
JOHN D. ROTHSCHILD

ARIZONA STATE UNIVERSITY, TEMPE

Virginia G Piper Center for Creative Writing, Global Studies Initiative
College of Public Programs at the ASU Downtown Phoenix Campus

Swartz, Beth Ames, 1936–
The Word in Paint / essays by Donald Kuspit, John D. Rothschild./
new poems by
Beckian Fritz Goldberg, Iliana Rocha, John Sparrow, Leah Soderberg;
foreward by Beckian Fritz Goldberg;
Includes poems by:
杜甫 (Du Fu, also Romanized as Tu Fu), 712–770 A.C.E., Chinese
李白 (Li Bai, also Romanized as Li Po), 701–762 A.C.E., Chinese
— 1st ed.

Published in conjunction with an exhibition
held at Arizona State University,
November 21–December 31, 2008
Includes bibliographic references.
ISBN 0-615-2222452450 (softcover)
1. Swartz, Beth Ames, 1936—Exhibitions
2. Spiritual life in art—Exhibitions
3. Poetry, Chinese
I. Kuspit, Donald II. Rothschild, John D.
III. Goldberg, Beckian Fritz. IV. Arizona State University. V. Title.

Frontispiece calligraphy by Kazuaki Tanahashi
Design by Michael Motley, Santa Fe

Printed in Singapore

■ Poems Inspired by the Paintings of Beth Ames Swartz

The Visual Text Project

FOREWORD BY BECKIAN FRITZ GOLDBERG

THE WORD IN PAINT is the result of a creative collaboration between the visual artist and the poet first inspired when the Virginia G Piper Center for Creative Writing at Arizona State University hosted a delegation from the University of Sichuan in Chengdu, China. Director of the Center's Global Studies Initiative, Jewell Parker Rhodes, introduced them to the work of Arizona artist Beth Ames Swartz who is nationally known and whose paintings were inspired by two of China's most revered poets, Du Fu and Li Bai. The members of the delegation were excited about the cultural and artistic dialogue in Swartz's work and enthusiastic about the possibilities of exploring the creative expression of community between ASU and Sichuan University through visual and poetic art.

With the support of Debra Friedman, Dean of ASU's School of Public Programs at the downtown Phoenix Campus, and Scott Muir, Director of the downtown campus library, Rhodes then sought the involvement of poets in the MFA Creative Writing Program at Arizona State University who would be teaching at the University of Sichuan as part of the Piper Global Studies Initiative.

Professor Beckian Fritz Goldberg, faculty member of ASU's MFA Creative Writing Program, two students from the Program, and Visiting Faculty John Sparrow from Royal Holloway College in England, viewed an exhibit of Swartz's paintings in Scottsdale, Arizona. In response, the poets wrote original poems based on particular works.

The fragments of text and the striking images combined in Swartz's paintings provided a unique dynamic, and the poets approached their responses in a number of remarkable ways. Who would have thought, for instance, a brief 8th century poem by Li Bai, *Zazen on Jingting Mountain*, would inspire the powerful and stark image of Swartz's painting, and both then in turn evoke for an American poet, thirteen centuries later, the events surrounding 9/11 in Goldberg's *Great Times*?

As a poet primarily interested in digital media, John Sparrow, wrote his response using procedural methods. Sparrow says, "Beth Ames Swartz's use of mixed media in her painting encourages a mixture of concrete reading and abstract viewing in which the visual qualities of the text (spatial placement and implied movement, opacity, noise) inform how the semantics of those fragments is interpreted within the wider context of the painting as a whole." Working with these ideas, Sparrow used Flash to break apart and visually reconstruct the language of translated Du Fu poems. This allowed him to situate his writing in relation to the problems often encountered by translators of Chinese poetry. The result is a partially improvised, reactionary compositional method which creates frequently unexpected themes, tension, ambiguities that retain the synesthetic approach possible when reading/viewing Swartz's paintings. Sparrow's digital version can be viewed at: http://www.asu.edu/pipercw center/global_outreach/locations/china/projects/dufu_swartz/sparrow/index.html

We hope *The Word in Paint* will continue to enrich members of the global community and to demonstrate the power of the arts to speak about the human experience across cultures.

Balancing Painting and Poetry: Beth Ames Swartz's Spiritual Art

DONALD KUSPIT

BETH AMES SWARTZ WANTS TO BALANCE PAINTING AND POETRY—generally philo-mystical poetry, ranging from the Torah and T. S. Eliot to Tu Fu and Li Po (among many others)—which is not to say that she wants to blur the difference between them, but rather that she wants each to amplify and reinforce the meaning and purpose of the other. She wants to establish expressive parity between them, rather than, as Horace advised, have painting follow the lead of poetry, as though the verbal was superior—certainly more discursive—than the visual. Painting, after all, appeals to only one sense—the sense of sight, however much the hand of the painter appeals to the sense of touch (without entirely satisfying it, because one cannot touch a painting with one's own hand, only see the painting, and the artist's touch, which exists at a visual remove)—while poetry is full of mindfulness, however mediated by words, playfully charged with instinct. So Swartz wants to make passionately mindful paintings—paintings in which sight becomes visionary insight, what is seen suddenly conveys what can only be seen with the mind's eye.

For purists, one can't mix painting and poetry—visual and verbal aesthetics—without compromising both. If "ripeness is all," as Shakespeare wrote, then each can only ripen on its own. But such insularity—self-limitation masquerading as autonomy—eventually becomes sterile and stultifying, as post-painterly abstraction makes clear: abstraction has lost the passion that made it paradoxically mindful and transcendental. Swartz's painting is primed with passion, as

9

the hyper-expressive surfaces of *The Thirteenth Moon Series* (2006-2008) indicate. Vigorously worked and re-worked, her very material surfaces flow with gestural force, as though driven by an irresistible current. However unstable its rhythm may seem, and whether it informs the sea or the mountains—the same elemental rhythm appears in *Evening Near Serpent River*, 2007 and *If I Could Walk on Ice, with My Feet Bare!*, 2006—it gives the image an abstract momentum that transform it into an epiphany. It becomes "proof" of another realm of being—a realm that can only become manifest through intense art. Swartz professes a concern with spiritual healing, which means altering the state of consciousness as well as of the body. Swartz's paintings solve the "mind/body" problem by showing that there is none: the painterly body of her art is informed with mindful images. They have an uncanny, hallucinatory quality: Swartz's landscapes are as surreal as those Max Ernst painted in the Arizona desert, and the rich texture of her expressionistic paintings is a cousin of the bizarre texture of Ernst's frottage paintings. But her paintings seem much more fraught with what Freud called primary process—they are in fact a kind of process or action painting, that is, painting in which the act of painting is part of the process of self-creation—and are more unearthly, as a desert often seems to be. Her images emerge from the rhythmically differentiated flow of the paint—rhythm is innate to flow, and indicates that it is not aimless and random—to form a landscape of mystically meaningful elements.

The poetry that Swartz incorporates into her paintings—sometimes it appears on the picture frame, as in *War*, 2007, sometimes it drips down the page (in Chinese fashion) like a grand gesture, as in *A View of the Wilderness*, 2007, and sometimes it emanates from the moon, forming a radiant aura confirming its sacredness, as in *An Hour of Changing Scenes*, 2006—adds to their meaningfulness. The visual elements are meaningful and expressive in themselves, and so are the verbal elements; their intimacy adds another—an unexpected, unforeseen, uncanny—dimension of meaning and expression. Both the paintings and poems are spiritually intense and poignant—*The Mei-Pei Lake* and *Night in the House by the River*, both 2007 are striking examples—in themselves. But integrating them makes for a spiritual richness and emotional depth that neither by itself is capable of. Fertilizing each other, they form a fresh spiritual growth. To see the words circling around the moon and spreading into cosmic space in *Standing Alone*, 2006-2007 or emanating from the eye of the sky in *The Way Goes on Forever*, 2007 is to realize the mystery of creation in a way that the unpainted poem and the wordless painting alone could never achieve.

Swartz is ecumenical—virtually encyclopedic—in her use of spiritual literature, which is part of her creativity. Searching it, she is in effect searching for her deepest self. "I use word and/or myth-like visual elements from many philosophic and religious systems (including Native American healing practices, Buddhism, Christianity, Taoism, the I-Ching, Jewish mysticism as taught in the Cabala, and the *chakra* system of Hinduism) in order to facilitate communication with viewers on both conscious and unconscious levels," Swartz writes. I think she succeeds—her "word[s] in paint" (the word made painterly flesh) instantly communicate, all the more so because they seem to appear spontaneously, like desert mirages. She suggests that all these systems share the same spiritual principles and ideals, however different the cultures in which they originated. One is reminded of Lessing's play *Nathan the Wise*, which suggested that all religious roads—Christianity, Islam, and Judaism for Lessing—lead to the same God. Swartz makes the same enlightened point, and reminds us that today there are even more roads—more spiritual resources (thanks to the so-called information revolution).

It is perhaps a "New Age" position, but the world is ready for a new spiritual age—a spiritual revolution. Spiritualization is the final step of civilization, indeed, confirmation that a society is truly civilized rather than emotionally barbarian (at war with itself as well as other societies, as Swartz's *War* implies). I think Swartz wants her art to catalyze a new spiritual consciousness; it does not simply distill the spiritual consciousness of past ages. She is in a "postmodern" position: no one spiritual "style" is preferable to another. The issue is not to choose between them, as though one was inherently superior to the other, but rather to synthesize them with the hope of finding their "common sense." I think Swartz goes a long way toward doing so: she is a postmodern spiritualist, using the variety of spiritual traditions to make a universal point.

One last point. Swartz has said that she wants to "translate philosophical concepts into aesthetic visual experiences." Lu Chi, in Wen Fu (301-302 A.D.), said that the artistic problem is to get the "artistic form [to] reach the level of the meaning." Swartz's works raise the question whether a modern artistic form—surreal expressionism (automatist absorption in the medium for the sake of visionary experience)—can translate traditional spiritual meaning into unconsciously accessible terms. I think they do; her elemental handling and imagery suggest a primordial spirituality. But the larger question is whether the level of meaning can reach the level of the form—whether the philosophical concept is worthy of aesthetic trans-figuration. Swartz suggests that only spiritual concepts make for convincing aesthetic forms.

Introduction to the History, Poets and Poetry of Tang China

JOHN D. ROTHSCHILD

TANG TIMES China was one of the most extensive and powerful states on the planet during the Tang Dynasty (618–907 A.C.E.).[1]

The ruler of the state of Qin united the country in 221 B.C.E.; his name was the origin of the name China.[2] The state of Qin had as its capital Chang'an. Eight hundred years later at the beginning of the Tang dynasty, Chang'an still was the center of the universe, not only because the emperor and his court resided there, but also because of the increased centralization of power. Applicants for government office had to pass an examination system administered from the capital; all appointments to govern derived from the capital.

During the Tang years, Chang'an was the largest city in the world, with about one million people within its walls and another million outside them. Because of massive trade with other cultures, Chang'an became a meeting place of many cultures and religions; it was the destination of thousands of foreign Silk Road traders. [Today, we know Chang'an as Xi'an (or Sian) in Shǎnxī province; it is the city where the terracotta warriors were discovered in 1974 after being buried since 210 B.C.E.]

The Tang dynasty is known as the "golden age" of Chinese culture partially resulting from the absorption, synthesis and fusion of many foreign ideas, religions and arts into the Chinese worldview. The bulk of the cultural flowering occurred during the reign of Emperor Xuanzhong (r. 712-56).[3] A crucial event in the Tang occurred on December 16th, 755, when a brilliant era was brought to an abrupt end with the An Shi Rebellion.[4] The rebellion reached an inconclusive end in 763, eight years after it began.

One year before the rebellion began, China's population totaled almost 53 million. By 764, the population count fell to under 17 million persons.[5] The 68% reduction resulted both from actual deaths because of war as well as the inability of the census to account for the drifting refugees. Political and economic havoc resulting from the rebellion led to a diminishing of central authority and long decline in the fortunes of the dynasty.

TANG POETS · In the realm of the aesthetic, especially in art and poetry, China of the Tang attained a level previously never approached. Buddhism in China reached its acme and joined with other forces in stimulating an outburst of expressing emotions through art and poetry.

The two greatest poets of the Tang illustrate two strands of Chinese thought, while another great Tang poet (who also was a painter) reflects a third strand:

杜甫	Du Fu (a.k.a. Tu Fu)	712-770 A.C.E.	Confucianism
李白	Li Bai (a.k.a. Li Po)	701-762 A.C.E.	Daoism
王维	Wang Wei	701-761 A.C.E.	Buddhism

Li Bai and Du Fu may be seen as opposites that complement one another—the *yin* and *yang* of poetry. Li Bai was a dynamic, fun-loving, outgoing free-spirit; Du Fu was a controlled, family-oriented, socially conscious member of society. Li Bai refused to take the *jinshi*, the "presented scholar examination," which was a passport to official service; Du Fu failed twice.

LI BAI · Li Bai was an outsider from the viewpoint of the higher echelons of Chinese society. Brought up about one hundred miles northeast of modern Chengdu in Sichuan province, he already was writing poetry and "courting the favor of the great" by age 14. His life took a completely new turn when he began living in the mountains as a recluse; in a letter he claims, "For several years I never set foot in any town."

Li Bai wandered his entire life; in spite of marrying four times, he roamed about the empire never setting-up his own household. He drank continually and to excess. He acquired numerous concubines and prostitutes, demonstrated a capacity for loyal friendships, and composed exciting poetry. He was a legend in his own time.

A lover of detachment and freedom, Li Bai's poems are Zen-like in their appreciation for the immediacy of experience, for their ability to live in the here-and-now. While Li's poetry demonstrates a Buddhist understanding of life's fragile and transient nature; nevertheless, he studied Daoism extensively and focused his poetry on the present. Li Bai was famous for his ability to compose poetry extemporaneously, even when drunk.

DU FU · Du Fu came from a good family, but one that was no longer well-to-do. He grew up, married, became devoted to his wife, and struggled to support his family. Like Li Bai, he wandered all over China, sometimes by choice, but more often fleeing violence or seeking a job. His poverty at times was so severe that one son died of starvation. Over the years, his health deteriorated so that by the end he suffered from malaria, lung disease and deafness. Because Du Fu lived in fateful times, his personal experiences gave him larger themes. Nearly forgotten at his death, he was rediscovered 40 years later. Stephen Owen, a scholar of Chinese poetry, says:

Du Fu is the greatest Chinese poet. His greatness rests on the consensus of more than a millennium of readers and on the rare coincidence of Chinese and Western literary values. Within the Chinese poetic tradition Du Fu is almost beyond judgment, because, like Shakespeare in our own tradition, his literary accomplishment has itself become a major component in the historical formation of literary values.[6]

Du Fu mastered of all Chinese poetic forms. His poetry (like Li's) is permeated with the Buddhist notion of the brevity of life, yet his poetry is less about celebrating experience than it is about the tragedy of human suffering. Du Fu sees things clearly; he keeps one eye on the present and the other on history. His greatness is the compassionate recognition of the trials of existence. His empathy for others marks him; he is our mirror into Tang times, reflecting everything—the turbulent, the poignant and the painful.

TANG POETRY · The traditional Chinese character for poem or poetry is 诗 (*shī*); this character is composed of two parts: 言 (*yán*) and 寺 (*sì*). The radical 言 means "words" or "speech." The phonetic element, 寺 (*sì*, temple, court), originally was written as 志 (*zhì*, purpose, will), suggesting a meaning of temple language of great feeling. Thus, the character 诗 suggests that poetry is the speech of the will, of the soul.

An early definition of poetry can be found in Mao's preface to the *Book of Odes* (詩经, *ShīJīng*): "When it is in the heart, it is *zhì*, when *zhì* is expressed in words, it is poetry."

Modern/recent-style poetry (近体诗, *jìntǐshī*), now known as regulated verse, can be traced as far back as the Six Dynasties (220–589 A.C.E.) when rules governing the tone and rhythm of Chinese characters were established. However, it was not until the Tang Dynasty that regulated verse was fully developed and adopted as a popular form in Chinese classical poetry.

Regulated verse (律诗, *lüshi*) consists of eight lines of five or seven syllables set in accordance with strict tonal patterns. Truncated verse (绝句, *juéjù* or *chüehchü*) omits four of the lines but maintains the tonal qualities of regulated verse.

Regulated verse conforms to rules governing tonal patterns and to the structure of its content. English translations cannot convey the required patterns embedded in the original.

Additionally, regulated verse requires parallelism between second and third couplets with strict antithesis, meaning that every pair of characters in order in each couplet is syntactically parallel.

In summary, the regulated verse of Du Fu and Li Bai may be characterized as an art form that is condensed, compressed, suggestive, and allusive and one whose tonal qualities and structural requirements do not translate readily into English.

NOTES

1. After Common Era (and Before Common Era), a dating system perhaps more sensitive to non-Western history and sensibilities.

2. The emperor now known as Qin Shi Huang or "First Emperor of the Qin Dynasty" applied the family name, Qin, to the area he governed, the state of Qin, and then to the larger area that Qin controlled; his given name was "Zhao Zheng" a.k.a. "Ying Zheng."

3. Commonly called Minghuang or "Brilliant Emperor."

4. Combining the family names of the two most prominent rebel generals, An Lu-shan and Shi-Siming, both of whom later were killed by their sons. In English, the event often is labeled the An Lu-shan rebellion. The history leading to the rebellion is fascinating. The emperor became infatuated with one concubine, Yang Guifei a.k.a. Lady Yang, who arranged for a distant cousin, Yang Guozhong, to become Chief Minister. Their increasing power led to conflict with other major political figures. After the rebellion began and the emperor fled Chang'an, imperial guards executed Yang Guozhong and forced the emperor to have Yang Guifei strangled.

5. Hung, William. *Tu Fu: China's Greatest Poet*. Cambridge: Harvard University Press, 1952, 202.

6. Owen, Stephen. *The Great Age of Chinese Poetry: The High Tang*. New Haven: Yale University Press, 1980, 183.

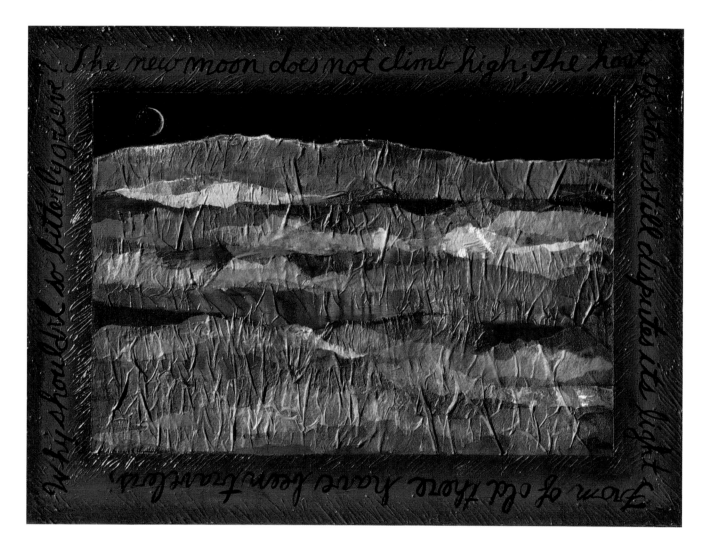

THE THIRTEENTH MOON: Ch'eng-tu City

acrylic and mixed media on canvas   36 × 48 inches (0.91m × 1.22m)   2007

Philosophy and Poetry in the Art of Beth Ames Swartz

JOHN D. ROTHSCHILD

AN UNDERSTANDING OF THE PHILOSOPHY underlying the paintings of Beth Ames Swartz enhances the viewing experience, especially for someone like Swartz whose career spans fifty years, includes a 2002 retrospective at Phoenix Art Museum as well as receiving the highest award in the State of Arizona for an artist (the Governor's Arts Award), and enjoys other professional achievements that include a solo exhibition at The Jewish Museum, NY, over eighty other one-person museum and gallery shows as well as two books and many catalogs, articles and videos documenting her accomplishments.

ORDERING, DISORDERING, REORDERING   The concept of ordering, disordering, and reordering is central to the art of Swartz. Scientists conceive of order and randomness, of entropy, and of eternity's eventual end when all differences disappear. Yet, Swartz is an optimist. She views life as an anti-entropic force for order. In her work, she constantly proposes an endless cycle of life, death, and rebirth rather than a seeming duality of life and death.

Her most recent series, *The Thirteenth Moon*, may be interpreted as a reminder of life's continuous renewal, since the thirteenth moon may bridge the last portion of an old year with the first portion of the new. (Interestingly, this recent series focuses on Chinese language and culture wherein the worldview usually consists of a complimentary, balancing dualism—such as the concept of *yin* and *yang*.)

Throughout all her series, Swartz says she explores systems of knowledge by translating philosophical concepts into aesthetic visual experiences. She works in series, beginning a new series—usually using an entirely different visual approach—after she solves the aesthetic challenges of her then current series.

Her paintings honor differences among cultures by utilizing symbols and words that represent concepts shared by people of widely different philosophic worldviews. She envisions that, by exposing people to the beliefs of others and by showing the interconnectedness of one belief system to another, each of us may experience a common compassion. Swartz studies systems of knowledge, both ones well known and those more esoteric; her art evolves from the process of incorporating these teachings into her life.

Swartz investigates the healing potential of images in all her series, often employing pilgrimage and other ritualistic acts in the creation processes. She uses words and/or myth-like visual elements from many philosophic and religious systems; her use of words and/or symbols within the context of painting intends to facilitate communication with viewers on both conscious and unconscious levels.

THE WORD IN PAINT Beginning in 1993, Swartz first inserted visually identifiable poetry into her series, *A Verse for the Eleventh Hour* (fig. 1) using a famous poem by William Butler Yeats: *The Second Coming.*

Swartz uses poetry within her art in order to help gain appreciation of a belief system that may appear different or alien to her intended viewing audience. The title, *The Word in Paint*, (first used by art critic John Perreault [3]) is a double-entendre in the sense that Swartz integrates words of poetry into her work, but her subject is philosophy, a meaning perhaps implied in the English language when we capitalize "word" to become "Word."

"Word" with a capital "W" suggests "Logos," a concept Heraclitus of Ephesus established in Western philosophy in about 500 B.C.E.[4] as meaning both the source and fundamental order underlying the universe. The title, *The Word in Paint*, may be best translated into Chinese as "philosophy conveyed in painting" (绘画中的哲学).

20

A Verse for the Eleventh Hour:
Fragment 1
acrylic, gold leaf and mixed media on handmade paper
18 × 23 inches (0.46m × 0.58m)   1993

A Verse for the Eleventh Hour: Fragment 3
acrylic, gold leaf and mixed media on handmade paper
18 × 23 inches (0.46m × 0.58m)   1993

Turning and turning in the widening gyre
The falcon cannot hear the falconer;
Things fall apart; the centre cannot hold;
Mere anarchy is loosed upon the world,[2]

Surely some revelation is at hand;
Surely the Second Coming is at hand.
The Second Coming! Hardly are those words out
When a vast image out of Spiritus Mundi
Troubles my sight [2]

Figure 1 (a)–(d)

A Story for the Eleventh Hour:
And the lotos rose quietly, quietly
acrylic and mixed media on shaped canvas
48 × 36 inches (1.22m × 0.91m) 1993

Dry the pool, dry concrete, brown edged,
And the pool was filled with water out of sunlight,
And the lotos rose, quietly, quietly,
The surface glittered out of heart of light,
And they were behind us, reflected in the pool.
Then a cloud passed, and the pool was empty.[5]

The word "lotos" is a variant of "lotus," an aquatic plant that, though it has roots in the mud, blossoms beautifully in the world above. Thus, the lotus is a symbol of purity and perfection because it grows out of mud but is not defiled by it, just as Buddha is born into the world but lives above the world.

Eliot's deliberate use of the variant "lotos" plays on the word "Logos," a word that denotes both the cosmic reason of Greek philosophy and, for some, the Christian will of God. In Buddhism and Hinduism, the lotus represents a symbol for elevation to the last chakra, the attainment of spiritual awakening and enlightenment, the transformation to nirvana.

A Story for the Eleventh Hour:
Reconciled among the stars
acrylic and mixed media on shaped canvas
39.5 × 30 inches (1.00m × 0.76m) 1993

Garlic and sapphires in the mud
Clot the bedded axle-tree.
The trilling wire in the blood
Sings below inveterate scars
Appeasing long forgotten wars.
The dance along the artery
The circulation of the lymph
Are figured in the drift of stars
Ascend to summer in the tree
We move above the moving tree
In light upon the figured leaf
And hear upon the sodden floor
Below, the boarhound and the boar
Pursue their pattern as before
But reconciled among the stars.[5]

The poetry and painting depict life's paradox, a force rooted in the earth but looking heavenward. Life feeds on life, yet life creates order from chaos.

Swartz pictures a universe where each star in the heaven(s) represents an enlightened being. The image visualizes a postulate of philosopher Rupert Sheldrake; this postulate (a morphogenetic field and The Hundred Monkey Theory) theorizes that all humans will move to Buddha-consciousness if 200,000 people achieve a state of enlightenment.

Figure 2 (a)–(b)

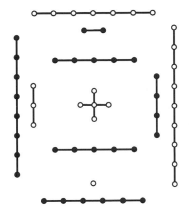

Yellow River Map

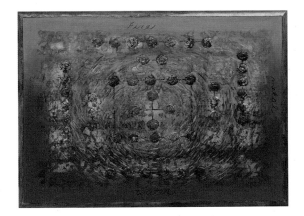

States of Change: #2
acrylic, gold leaf and mixed media on shaped canvas
36 × 48 inches (1.22m × 0.91m) 1999

Five symbolic entities, often translated into English as "elements," are known in Chinese as 五行 (wǔ xíng) and more appropriately interpreted as "five states of change" or "five forces." The five states of change are: water, fire, wood, metal and earth. These five states of change also have correspondences to the five cardinal points and the five seasons, the center (earth) being added to the West's traditional four directions/seasons.

States of Change: Om Mani #4
acrylic, gold leaf and mixed media on shaped canvas
48 × 60 inches (1.22m × 1.52m) 1998–99

ཨོཾ་མ་ཎི་པ་དྨེ་ཧཱུྃ

This phrase is a variant of the Sanskrit phrase:
Om Mani Padme Hum.
(唵嘛呢叭咪吽, Ǎn Mání Bāmī Hōng)

A literal English translation would be, "Om, jewel-in-the-lotus, Hum"; in other words, two syllables ("Om" and "Hum") enclosed by so-called "seed-syllables" that mean "jewel-in-the-lotus." The intended meaning equates the Buddhist concept of a "jewel" as an enlightened mind that flowers from the "lotus" of human consciousness.

Figure 3 (a)–(d)

A related series, *A Story for the Eleventh Hour* (1993, fig. 2), includes words and symbols within the paintings and, importantly, references to the poetry of T. S. Eliot, particularly *Burnt Norton* and *The Waste Land*.

In her next series, *Shen Qi* (神气) (1996–1999) and its closely related, subsequent series, *States of Change* (五行) (1999–2001), Swartz paints works with symbols that allude to sources of human wisdom including:

- Book of Changes (易经, *Yi Jīng* or *I Ching*)
- Yellow River Map (河图, *Hé Tú*)
- *Cabala*, the *Tree of Life* and the *Cabalistic Scheme of the Four Worlds*
- The chakra system of *kundalini-yoga*
- The Sanskrit phrase OM MANI PADME HUM

In *Shen Qi* and *States of Change* (fig. 3) paintings, the order of square sheets of gold, disordered by random destruction by the artist, are reordered into a grid that seduces the eye with its seeming reality, but the alluring gold represents a metaphorical illusion, a trick of the *Maya*[6]; Swartz paints the "real" reality, words of enduring value shinning jewel-like from behind the gold.

In her next two series, *Visible Reminders* (2002–2003) and *Tree of Life* (2002), Swartz incorporates phrases and symbols from, Cabala[7] and the bible into her paintings (fig. 4).

Swartz titles all paintings from the series *The Fire and the Rose* (2003–2005) with words from *Little Gidding* (one of *The Four Quartets* by T. S. Eliot) and she purposely hides lines of poetry from *Little Gidding*[9] within the central area of the large paintings (fig. 5).

From late 2005, a new series began evolving wherein words shift from the central painted area to the border of the painted frame; at the same time Swartz's earlier use of (primarily) abstract images transforms into a new style of surreal expressionistic landscapes that evoke emotion and thought using color and form in a manner different from those employed by more realist painters.

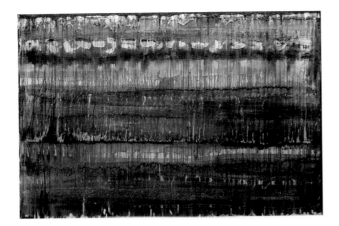

Visible Reminders: There Is a Time
acrylic on canvas
48 × 72 inches (1.22m × 1.83m)   2002

Tree of Life: #1, Keter
acrylic and paste on canvas
30 × 30 inches (0.76m × 0.76m)   2002

To every thing there is a season, and a time to every purpose under the heaven: [3]

Many believe Ecclesiastes contains the most beautiful "poetry" found in the Old Testament.

Ernest Hemingway used a different portion of Ecclesiastes (1.5) for the title of his first significant novel: "The sun also ariseth, and the sun goeth down, and hasteth to his place where he arose."

Cabala is an ancient Jewish philosophy built upon a tradition of mystical interpretation of Scripture. The map describing cabala is called the Tree of Life; it is composed of ten "numbers" or "spheres."

Keter is the highest of these spheres (Sephiroth in Hebrew). When we experience this realm, all separateness and fragmentation are gone; all is one.

Figure 4 (a)–(d)

The Fire and the Rose:
Being between two lives
acrylic on canvas   60 × 60 inches (1.52m × 1.52m)   2003

The Fire and the Rose:
I pray you to forgive both bad and good
acrylic on canvas   48 × 60 inches (1.22m × 1.52m)   2004

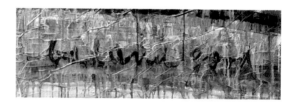

There are three conditions which often look alike
Yet differ completely, flourish in the same hedgerow:
Attachment to self and to things and to persons, detachment
From self and from things and from persons; and, growing
Between them indifference
Which resembles the others as death resembles life,
Being between two lives—unflowering, between
The live and the dead nettle. This is the use of memory:
For liberation—not less of love but expanding
Of love beyond desire, and so liberation
From the future as well as the past.9

These things have served their purpose: let them be.
So with your own, and pray they be forgiven
By others, as I pray you to forgive
Both bad and good. Last season's fruit is eaten
And the full-fed beast shall kick the empty pail.
For last year's words belong to last year's language
And next year's words await another voice.9

Figure 5 (a)–(d)

This new series, *The Thirteenth Moon* (fig. 6) continues including "the word in paint," using lines from a poem by William Butler Yeats, *The Phases of the Moon* [10]. Note, the words purposely are almost illegible once again even though their location shifted to the border area.

IN WHAT MANNER MAY THE WORD BE VISUALIZED?   Ancient tradition requires that the name of God not be written. Many other faiths preach that the name of God not be used in an inappropriate manner.

Most frequently, Swartz hides symbols or the "word/Word" in the sense that a viewer may recognize some seemingly decipherable message appears within the visual field; yet, even when individual words or symbols may be discerned, the entire message may not be consciously comprehended.

One reason for hiding words, phrases and symbols behind paint is that Swartz believes art acts on the Jungian [11] unconsciousness, conscious knowledge not being required. Viewers may recognize a message lays buried behind the paint, but that message remains unreadable in its entirety, even when examined closely. Anyone who consciously tries to "get the message" will not. Yet, in this striving, Swartz believe viewers will succeed unconsciously.

Allowing words to become more apparent raises the possibility that viewers/readers holding one belief system may feel that art alluding to a different belief system confronts their personal beliefs. Swartz feels that, when she allows words to be visually recognizable in a painting, using poetry (rather than quoting wisdom from a specific belief system) conveys the message in an acceptable, non-confrontational manner. Swartz hopes that literally visualizing the word as she has in recent work echoes the great Islamic calligraphic tradition wherein the Word is visualized.

The Thirteenth Moon: All thought becomes an image
acrylic and mixed media on canvas
36 × 48 inches (0.91m × 1.22m)   2005

The Thirteenth Moon: Beyond the visible world
acrylic and mixed media on canvas
36 × 48 inches (0.91m × 1.22m)   2005

All thought becomes an image and the soul
Becomes a body: that body and that soul
Too perfect [10]

Too lonely for the traffic of the world:
Body and soul cast out and cast away
Beyond the visible world. [10]

Figure 6 (a)–(d)

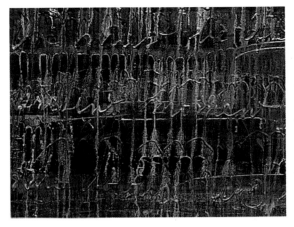

Fig 7 (a) Visible Reminders: Muted Light
acrylic on canvas   48 × 60 inches (1.22m × 1.52m)   2001

Fig 7 (a) We must be fully alive in the present moment to experience the divine.

FRAMES, GRIDS AND GESTURES Swartz began employing painted frames with *A Story for the Eleventh Hour* (1993) by applying material along the edge of the shaped canvas used in this series. The "painted frame" reinforces the intended themes of cosmological and spiritual journeys of being by creating a window from which the viewer may look outward onto the universe and inward into themselves.

She continued using shaped canvas and golden-edged "frames" with *Shen Qi* (1996–1997) and *States of Change* (1999–2000); however, she began organizing the central area of the painting as a grid.[12] The golden "squares" applied in grid fashion create order, an order that is counterbalanced by the chaos and randomness of the disorder created by violating the form of the individual golden squares.

With the series *Visible Reminders* (2001–2002), Swartz again creates a grid of seeming order by hiding words in horizontal lines along with horizontal bands of color that then are further ordered (and disordered) by vertical, seemingly random, drips (fig. 7).

Shen Qi:
The Cabalistic Scheme of the Four Worlds #3
mixed media with gold leaf on shaped canvas
36 × 48 inches (0.91m × 1.22m) 1997

The outer, painted frame of gold leaf over the shaped canvas creates an appearance of order as do concentric circles and the grid of six by four gold "squares." The gold squares, however, are composed of very chaotic smaller pieces. Overall, the painting conveys an image of ordering, disordering and reordering.

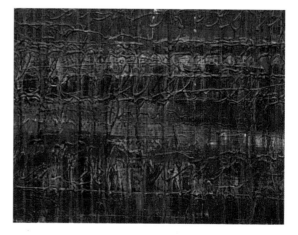

Visible Reminders:
The Still Point of the Turning Wheel
acrylic on canvas 40 × 60 inches (1.22m × 1.52m) 2001–2

Order created by horizontal bands of color over horizontal words. Disorder created by seemingly random vertical drips. Reordering created by the grid formed by the horizontal and vertical elements.

Figure 8 (a) – (d)

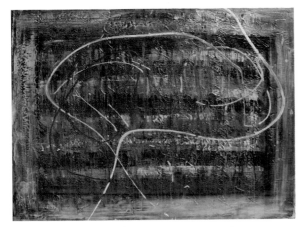

Figure 9(a) The Fire and the Rose: While the light fails on a winter's afternoon, in a secluded chapel *acrylic on canvas 36" × 48" (0.91m × 1.22m) 2002–4*

Figure 9(b) *Fluid, gestured strokes violate the order imposed by the painted frame "freeing" the interior grid thereby re-establishing an ongoing dialogue between ordering, disordering and reordering.*

Swartz abandons use of painted frames in her *Visible Reminders* series; but soon thereafter she returns to using painted frames, both as a device for creating order and as a method for simultaneously focusing attention inward, on our private thoughts, and outward to the exterior world. By the time of *The Fire and the Rose* series (fig. 9), Swartz uses the painted frame to bind and to order the apparently "disordered central window" (where, in a painting paradox, the seeming order created by horizontal "rows" of hidden words and horizontal paint strokes may be disordered by seemingly random vertical drips). She now breaches the seeming order imposed by the painting's division into painted frame and central window by using flowing brush strokes connecting "frame" and "window," thereby breaking intentionally her labored illusion of ordered separation of exterior and interior realities.

Swartz continues evolving her use of painted frames and grids in latest *The Thirteenth Moon* series; words now move from central window to outer frame and from purposely illegible to purposely legible. As the series progresses, she abandons the painted frames technique and begins inserting words that are neither immediately legible nor illegible, but small enough not to impinge on the painting's overall aesthetic power.

SUMMARY   In summary, a review of Swartz's career captures the spirit of a visual artist repeatedly reinventing her art by finding philosophical solace from multicultural sources, especially poetic ones, yet reinventing with a continuing focus on her ever evolving attempt at convincing viewers that we are all one. Swartz believes in the healing power of art, whether visual, auditory or written. All things change, yet some human truths remain constant; to quote a favorite poem of Swartz:

> *Words, after speech, reach*
> *Into the silence. Only by the form, the pattern,*
> *Can words or music reach*
> *The stillness, as a Chinese jar still*
> *Moves perpetually in its stillness.*[13]

NOTES:

1. Yeats, W.B. *Michael Robartes and the Dancer*, Churchtown, Dundrum: The Cuala Press, 1920, *The Second Coming*, lines 1–4.

2. Ibid., lines 9–13.

3. *The Fire and the Rose*. Exh. cat. Vanier Galleries, Scottsdale, AZ and Aspen International Art, Aspen, CO, 2003. Essay (*Beth Ames Swartz: The Word in Paint*) by John Perreault. 22pp. 20 colorplates.

4. Use of B.C.E. (Before Common Era) and A.C.E. (After Common Era) recognizes some cultures may appreciate a dating system perhaps more sensitive to non-Western sensibilities.

5. Eliot, T. S. *The Complete Poems and Plays 1909-1950*, (New York: Harcourt, Brace and Company, 1952), *Four Quartets: Burnt Norton*, I, 118 and II, 119.

6. Maya: (Sanskrit), in Hinduism, Maya is to be seen through, like an epiphany, in order to achieve *moksha* (liberation of the soul from the cycle of *samsara*, the cycle of reincarnation and rebirth).

7. Cabala, the correct English spelling of *Kabbalah*, which literally means "receiving," is the mystical aspect of Judaism.

8. Bible, *Ecclesiastes* (3.1).

9. Eliot, op. cit., *Four Quartets: Little Gidding*, III, 142 and II, 141.

10. Yeats, William Butler. *The Wild Swans at Coole*. 1919: from "35. The Phases of the Moon" lines 60–62 and 63–65

11. Carl Gustav Jung (1875-1961, Swiss) who emphasized understanding the psyche through exploring the worlds of dreams, art, mythology, world religion and philosophy.

12. Renaissance artists used a grid to establish perspective based upon projecting the grid plane to a single vanishing point, thereby helping artists make a painting look more life-like, more real; for many, the grid made the world feel more ordered, more susceptible to control. Many modern artists use a grid as a way of reminding themselves and viewers that a painting is not real; it is not a projection of visual reality. Maurice Denis (1870–1943, French) was among the first modern artist to insist on the flatness of the picture plane—one of the great starting points for modernism, as practiced in the visual arts. In his famous proposal for the definition of painting, offered in 1890, Denis stated: "Remember that a picture, before being a battle horse, a nude, an anecdote or whatnot, is essentially a flat surface covered with colors assembled in a certain order." Denis is an interesting person for another reason too; in 1898, he produced a theory of creation that found the source for art in the character of the painter: "That which creates a work of art is the power and the will of the artist."

13. Eliot, op. cit., *Four Quartets: Burnt Norton*, 121.

杜甫　DU FU, also Romanized as Tu Fu, 712–770 A.C.E., Chinese

旅夜書懷	*A Night Abroad*
細草微風岸	A light wind is rippling at the grassy shore…
危檣獨夜舟	Through the night, to my motionless tall mast,
星垂平野闊	The stars lean down from open space,
月湧大江流	And the moon comes running up the river.
名豈文章著	If only my art might bring me fame
官應老病休	And free my sick old age from office! –
飄飄何所似	Flitting, flitting, what am I like
天地一沙鷗	But a sand-snipe in the wide, wide world!

Translation Selected
Bynner, Witter and Kiang Kang-Hu, trans. *The Jade Mountain: A Chinese Anthology (Being 300 Poems of the Tang Dynasty (618-906)*. New York: Alfred A Knopf, 1929, renewal copyright 1957; Vintage Books, 1972, no. 113, 152.

Other English Translations
At least twenty-five additional English translations exist including:
Fletcher (1919), Ayscough & Lowell (1934), Hung (1952), Rexroth (1956), Alley (1962), Davis (1962), Hawkes (literal character-by-character version, 1965), Hawkes (prose version, 1965), Birch (1965), Watson (1971), Cooper (1973), Herdan (1973), Hart (1974), Liu & Lo (1975), Wu (1981), Seaton (1982), Hinton (1988), Mc Craw (1992), Seth (1993), Hamill (1993), Barnstone & Chou (2005), Seaton (2006), Holyoak (2007), Kline (not dated, c. 2000-8), and Tao (not dated, c. 2000-8).

THE THIRTEENTH MOON: And the moon comes running up the river

acrylic and mixed media on canvas   30 × 30 inches (0.76m × 0.76m)   2006

李白　LI BAI, also Romanized as Li Po, 701–762 A.C.E., Chinese

長相思之一	*Endless Yearning I*
長相思	I am endlessly yearning
在長安	To be in Changan.
絡緯秋啼金井闌	…Insects hum of autumn by the gold brim of the well;
微霜淒淒簟色寒	A thin frost glistens like little mirrors on my cold mat;
孤燈不明思欲絕	The high lantern flickers; and deeper grows my longing.
卷帷望月空長歎	I lift the shade and, with many a sigh, gaze upon the moon,
美人如花隔雲端	Single as a flower, centred from the clouds.
上有青冥之長天	Above, I see the blueness and deepness of sky.
下有淥水之波瀾	Below, I see the greenness and the restlessness of water….
天長路遠魂飛苦	Heaven is high, earth wide; bitter between them flies my sorrow.
夢魂不到關山難	Can I dream through the gateway, over the mountain?
長相思	Endless longing
摧心肝	Breaks my heart.

Translation Selected
Bynner, Witter and Kiang Kang-Hu, trans. *The Jade Mountain: A Chinese Anthology (Being 300 Poems of the Tang Dynasty (618-906).*
New York: Alfred A Knopf, 1929, renewal copyright 1957; Vintage Books, 1972, no. 80, 69.

Other English Translations
Fletcher, W. J. B. *More Gems of Chinese Verse.* Shanghai: Commercial Press Limited, 1919, 33-4.
Online: http://www.archive.org/details/gemsofchinesever00fletiala
Hamill, Sam. *Crossing the Yellow River: 300 Poems from the Chinese.* Rochester, NY: BOA Editions, 2000, 78-9.

THE THIRTEENTH MOON: Heaven is high, earth wide; bitter between them flies my sorrow

acrylic and mixed media on canvas 30 × 30 inches (0.76m × 0.76m) 2006

Breakup of Pangaea

Bacteria equal continents. A cartographer approaches the heart,
finds pigeons, each one the shape & color of my individual sorrows:
a moth pinned to felt, half a cactus.

I watch a purple & fingerless sunset travel
from a bird tail, then to its chest. Then it flies away
to another white crumb

like the one in my fingernail. Someone said the curious
speck in the center of a fingernail means someone loves you.
I waiting for someone to reveal himself, for love not to be so goddamn

anonymous, to spit in my eye like a llama.

—*Iliana Rocha*

❖ Responding to the painting *Heaven is high, earth wide; bitter between them flies my sorrow* (page 37)

Great Times

1.

The birds wear black hoods like
Abu Ghraib. What are we to do?

Love is poison they say.
I say it's more like a dog

sniffing your privacy. Except
for the photographs.

2.

The sky is *empty*. No,
empty. You sense the airplanes

aren't there. As I drove to work,
I noted flags half-mast and

I thought only someone had died.

3.

Night pours in like two waterfalls,
no good. It cannot blank
the blank.

The birds have vanished down
the sky like centuries.
When

Du Fu's son died of starvation,
Du Fu wrote a poem about
the government.

—*Beckian Fritz Goldberg*

❖ Responding to the painting *The birds have vanished down the sky* (page 41)

39

李白　LI BAI, also Romanized as Li Po, 701–762 A.C.E., Chinese

独坐敬亭山	*Zazen on Jingting Mountain*
众鸟高飞尽	The birds have vanished down the sky.
孤云独去闲	Now the last cloud drains away.
相看两不厌	We sit together, the mountain and me,
只有敬亭山	Until only the mountain remains.

Translation Selected

Hamill, Sam, trans. *Endless River*. New York: Weatherhill, Inc., 1993, 110.

Seaton, Jerome P. and Maloney, Dennis, eds. *A Drifting Boat*. New York: White Pine Press, 1994, 47 [using the title *Zazen on the Mountain*].

Hamill, Sam. *Crossing the Yellow River: 300 Poems from the Chinese*. Rochester, NY: BOA Editions, 2000, 94.

Hamill, Sam and Seaton, J. P., ed. & trans. *The Poetry of Zen*, Boston & London: Shambhala, 2004, 42.

Barnstone Tony and Chou, Ping, ed. & trans. *The Anchor Book of Chinese Poetry*. New York: Random House, Inc., 2005, 123.

Other English Translations

Giles, Herbert A., ed. *History of Chinese Literature*. New York: Frederick Ungar Publishing, 1901, 1967, 154.

Obata, Shigeyoshi. *The Works of Li Po, The Chinese Poet*. New York: E. P. Dutton & Co., 1922, 57.

Seaton, J. P. & Cryer, James, trans. *Bright Moon, Perching Birds: Poems*. Middletown, Connecticut: Wesleyan University Press, 1971, 1987, 9.

Liu, Wu-chi and Lo, Irving Yucheng, ed. *Sunflower Spendor: Three Thousand Years of Chinese Poetry*. New York: Anchor Books, 1975, 110.

Hinton, David, trans. *The Selected Poems of Li Po*. New York: New Directions Publishing Company, 1996, 67.

Owen, Stephen, trans., in Mack, Maynard, ed. *The Norton Anthology of World Masterpieces*. New York: W. W. Norton, 1997

Pine, Red (aka Porter, Bill). *Poems of the Masters: China's Classic Anthology of Tang and Sung Dynasty Verse*.

Port Townsend WA: Copper Canyon Press, 2004.

Holyoak, Keith, trans. *Facing the Moon: Poems of Li Bai and Du Fu*. Durham, NH: Oyster River, 2007, 50-1.

Anonymous and undated translation at http://www.poetseers.org/the_great_poets/li_po/li/alone_looking_at_the_mountain

THE THIRTEENTH MOON: The birds have vanished down the sky

acrylic and mixed media on canvas   36 × 48 inches (0.91m × 1.22m)   2006

杜甫　DU FU, also Romanized as Tu Fu, 712–770 A.C.E., Chinese

渼陂行

岑參兄弟皆好奇	攜我遠來遊渼陂
天地黯慘忽異色	波濤萬頃堆琉璃
琉璃汗漫泛舟入	事殊興極憂思集
鼉作鯨吞不復知	惡風白浪何嗟及
主人錦帆相為開	舟子喜甚無氛埃
鳧鷖散亂棹謳發	絲管啁啾空翠來
沈竿續縵深莫測	菱葉荷花淨如拭
宛在中流渤澥清	下歸無極終南黑
半陂以南純浸山	動影裊窕沖融間
船舷暝戛雲際寺	水面月出藍田關
此時驪龍亦吐珠	馮夷擊鼓群龍趨
湘妃漢女出歌舞	金支翠旗光有無
咫尺但愁雷雨至	蒼茫不曉神靈意
少壯幾時奈老何	向來哀樂何其多

The Waters of the Mei-Pei

Two friends whose love of wonders led them oft
To leave the haunts and scenes of every day,
Invited me to join them in a voyage
Across the waters of the dread Mei-Pei!

Where nature in her changeful moods is seen,
In grandeur and in terror side by side;
Where mighty forces alter heaven and earth,
And puny human strength and life deride.

Will countless billows of the wide expanse
In ceaseless motion mount and roll afar?
Through fluid piles of seeming crystal rocks
Will our boat sail beyond the sheltering bar?

Delightful is the venture that we take,
And yet dire fears will gather in our throat,
The gavial huge may come in search of prey,
The monster whales may overturn our boat! ▶

Translation Selected
Budd, Charles. *Chinese Poems*. London: Oxford University Press, 1912, 63-67. [Budd believed Mei-Pei Lake to be, "A vast body of water in some wild and remote part of the Empire, probably in the Northwest; but the exact locality is disputed."]
Budd's English "translation" is an original work of art, but not as nearly as accurate as those of Hung and Owen.

Other English Translations
Hung, William. *Tu Fu: China's Greatest Poet*. Cambridge: Harvard University Press, 1952, 53-4, XIX. [According to Hung, the Mei-Pei Lake was about twenty-four miles southwest of Chàng-an.]
Owen, Stephen. *The Great Age of Chinese Poetry: the High Tang*. New Haven and London: Yale University Press, 1981, 191-2.

The moon has risen and its silver [?]ness comes stealing soft[...]on [?] in beauty glow — while we sit idly on the [?]side and watch the nodding peaks in depths below

THE THIRTEENTH MOON: An hour of changing scenes

acrylic and mixed media on canvas   60 × 48 inches (1.52m × 1.22m)   2006

Fierce winds may rise and billows roll and break!
But our brave friends unloose the flowing sail,
And through the scattering flocks of duck and tern
The boat glides on—the white foam in our trail

The pure and bracing air inflates our lungs—
Afar from towns where dust with cleanness vies;
The boatmen chant gay ditties as they work,
While sounds of lutes rise to the azure skies.

As fresh as dew on early morning flowers
The leaves of water-lilies float around,
Upon the surface of the water clear,
Through which we peer in vain to find the ground.

Then yielding to the current, broad and strong,
Toward the central flood we quickly forge;
The waters pure as those of Puh and Hsiai,
Yet darkly deep as in the Chong-Nan gorge.

The mountain heights whose base abuts the lake
Are mirrored clearly in the southern end;
The Great Peace Temple, which in cloudland hangs
Reflects its image in the eastern bend.

The moon has risen, and its silver beams
Across the Lan-Tien Pass in beauty glow,
While we sit idly on the vessel's side
And watch the nodding peaks in depths below.

And as we view the mirage of the heights
Which tower in mighty strength above our heads,
The swift Li-Long in prodigal display
A shower of pearls upon the water spreads.

The Ruler of the Rivers beats his drum,
And dragons haste the summons to obey;
The Consorts of the ancient king descend,
Led by the Maiden of the Star-lit Way.

To branchèd instruments of beaten gold,
Adorned with pendants of sapphire and jade,
They sing, and dance, midst lights of many hues,
Which flash in splendour, then in darkness fade.

In ecstasy we watch the wondrous scene,
But awe and joy are mingled in our mind,
For now far off we hear the thunder peal,
And lowering clouds with lurid lights are lined.

The waters heave with burdensome unrest,
The air is full of shadows of the dead;
The Spirits of the Universe are near,
And we cannot divine their portents dread.

And such is life—an hour of changing scenes
Of fitful joy and quickly following grief;
An hour of buoyant youth in rapid flight,
And then old age to end life—sad and brief!

A Drawing of Spirits Ending

something alone and pure
sigh a battle
you are now angels
copies of ghosts
group flesh
I grieve and would forget
the poisonous song
always thinking and forgetting
now with the old
languid smile
officious and abruptly sobering

there are colors in the wind
lovelier than moon rising
venting beauty
the sky
a new sketching
silk thunder
so that even night
is art

—John Sparrow

❖ Responding to the painting *An hour of changing scenes* (page 43)

After All We Know

We have become restless as seeds.
Turning to the earth, we gather pieces
of it—leaves, found tufts of rabbit fur
to save in old shoe boxes, rusted tins.
We swallow what grows from land
like medicine, try to feel the quick light
through a needle eye over our hands.
Most days, death is forgotten,
told as time. We watch clouds pass
over the red sun, thin as gauze, words—
our wounds seeping through.

—Leah Soderberg

❖ Responding to the painting *The way goes on forever* (page 55)

杜甫　DU FU, also Romanized as Tu Fu, 712–770 A.C.E., Chinese

早秋苦热堆案相仍	*Too Much Heat, Too Much Work*
七月六日苦炎蒸 对食暂餐还不能	It's the fourteenth of August, and I'm too hot To endure food, or bed.
每愁夜中白足蝎 况乃秋后转多蝇	Steam and the fear of scorpions keep me awake. I'm told the heat won't fade with Autumn. Swarms of flies arrive.
束带发狂欲大叫 簿书何急来相仍	I'm roped into my clothes. In another moment I'll scream down the office As the paper mountains rise higher on my desk.
南望青松架短壑 安得赤脚蹋层冰	O those real mountains to the south of here! I gaze at the ravines kept cool by pines. If I could walk on ice, with my feet bare!

Translation Selected
Kizer, Carolyn Ashley, ed. *Carrying Over: Poems from the Chinese Urdu Macedonian Yiddish and French African*.
Port Townsend, WA: Copper Canyon Press, 1988, 29.

Other English Translations
Hung William. *Tu Fu: China's Greatest Poet*. Cambridge: Harvard University Press, 1952, 132, CIX.
Owen, Stephen. *The Great Age of Chinese Poetry: The High Tang*. New Haven: Yale University Press, 1980, 200-1.
Holyoak, Keith, trans. *Facing the Moon: Poems of Li Bai and Du Fu*. Durham, NH: Oyster River, 2007, 80-1.

THE THIRTEENTH MOON. If I could walk on ice, with my feet bare!

acrylic and mixed media on canvas 24 × 36 inches (0.61m × 0.91m) 2006

杜甫　DU FU, also Romanized as Tu Fu, 712–770 A.C.E., Chinese

獨立	*Standing Alone*
空外一鷙鳥	Empty skies. And beyond, one hawk.
河間雙白鷗	Between river banks, two white gulls
飄搖搏擊便	Drift and flutter. Fit for an easy kill,
容易往來游	To and fro, they follow contentment.
草露亦多濕	Dew shrouds grasses. Spiderwebs are still
蛛絲仍未收	Not gathered in. The purpose driving
天機近人事	Heaven become human now, I stand where
獨立萬端憂	Uncounted sorrows begin beginning alone.

Translation Selected

Hinton, David. *The Selected Poems of Tu Fu*. New York, New Directions Publishing Corporation, 1988, 1989, 46; Hinton translation also appears in: Weinberger, Eliot, ed. *The New Directions Anthology of Classical Chinese Poetry*. New York: New Directions Publishing Corporation, 2003, 2004, 107.

Other English Translations

Rexroth, Kenneth. *One Hundred Poems from the Chinese*. New York: New Directions Publishing Corporation, 1971, IV, 6.

Wu, Juntao, trans. *Tu Fu–a New Translation*. Hong Kong: The Commercial Press, Ltd., 1981, 68-9.

Hamill, Sam, trans. *Endless River*. New York: Weatherhill, Inc., 1993, 37.

Hamill, Sam. *Crossing the Yellow River: 300 Poems from the Chinese*. Rochester, NY: BOA Editions, 2000, 157.

Hamill, Sam and Seaton, J. P., ed. & trans. *The Poetry of Zen*, Boston & London: Shambhala, 2004, 51.

Owen, Stephen, trans. & ed. *An Anthology of Chinese Literature*. New York: W.W. Norton, 1996, 426.

Barnstone Tony and Chou, Ping, ed. & trans. *The Anchor Book of Chinese Poetry*. New York: Random House, Inc., 2005, 134.

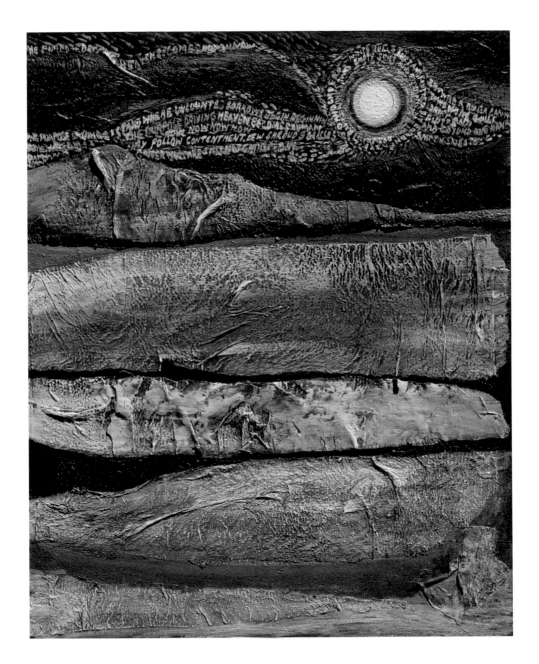

THE THIRTEENTH MOON: Standing Alone

acrylic and mixed media on canvas   20 × 16 inches (0.51m × 0.41m)   2006-2007

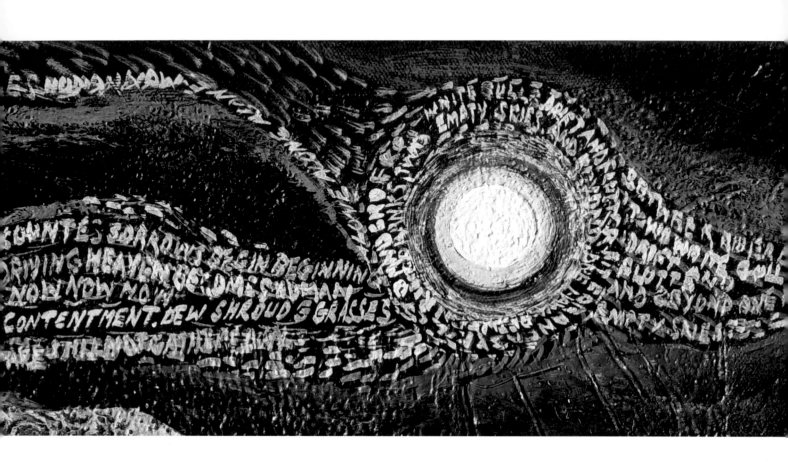

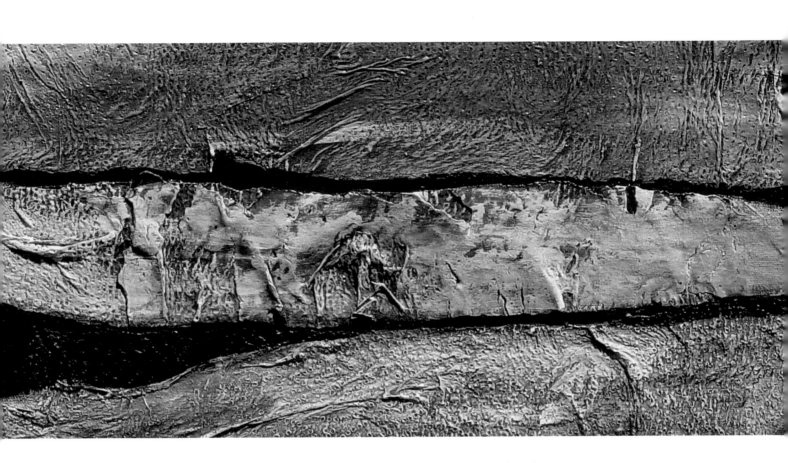

THE THIRTEENTH MOON: Standing Alone *(details)*

acrylic and mixed media on canvas   20 × 16 inches (0.51m × 0.41m)   2006-2007

杜甫　DU FU, also Romanized as Tu Fu, 712–770 A.C.E., Chinese

發秦州	*Departing from Ch'in-Chou*[1]
我衰更懶拙	As old age weakens me, I grow lazy and foolish.
生事不自謀	I make no plans for the future.
無食問樂土	Hungry, I remember a land of plenty:
無衣思南州	cold, I recall the warmth of the south.
漢源十月交	In early November, Han-yuan
天氣涼如秋	is cool and crisp like autumn,
草木未黃落	but leaves have not turned yellow and fallen,
況聞山水幽	and the landscape is still lovely.
栗亭名更佳	Chestnut Station promises good fortune,
下有良田疇	and the plains are thick with farms
充腸多薯蕷	growing delectable yams
崖蜜亦易求	and wild honey and
密竹復冬筍	forests of bamboo shoots. ▶

1. Qin-zhou
Translation Selected
Hamill, Sam. *Crossing the Yellow River: 300 Poems from the Chinese*. Rochester, NY: BOA Editions, 2000, 143-144.
[A slightly different version appeared in: Hamill, Sam, trans. Midnight Flute: Chinese Poems of Love and Longing.
New York: Shambhala, 1994, 54-6.

Other English Translations
Hung William. *Tu Fu: China's Greatest Poet*. Cambridge: Harvard University Press, 1952, 155, CCXLIX.
Alley, Rewi, trans. *Du Fu Selected Poems*. Beijing: Foreign Language Press, 1962, 2001, 164-7.
Davis, A(lbert) R(ichard). *Tu Fu*. New York: Twayne Publishers, Inc., 1971, 68-9. 90/6/4:
Han-yüan was a district of T'ung-ku—modern Ch'eng-hsien, Kansu.
Chou, Eva Shan. *Reconsidering Tu Fu: Literary Greatness and Cultural Context*. (Cambridge: Cambridge University Press, 1995, 1998 transferred to digital), 169: "His initial decision, it appears, consisted simply of quitting the Central Plains, with his actual destination undecided. In his first stop, at Ch'in-chou, to the west of Chang'an, he several times contemplated settling down. He did not do so, however, and went on to Ch'eng-tu."
Watson, Burton, trans. *The Selected Poems of Du Fu*. New York: Columbia University Press, 2002, 67-8.

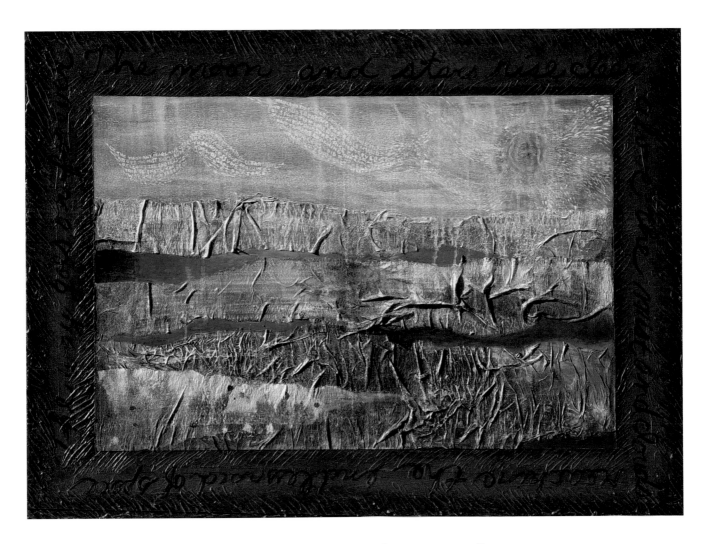

THE THIRTEENTH MOON: The way goes on forever

acrylic and mixed media on canvas   36 × 48 inches (0.91m × 1.22m)   2007

清池可方舟
雖傷旅寓遠
庶遂平生游
此邦俯要沖
實恐人事稠
應接非本性
登臨未銷憂
溪谷無異石
塞田始微收
豈復慰老夫
惘然難久留
日色隱孤戍
烏啼滿城頭
中宵驅車去
飲馬寒塘流
磊落星月高
蒼茫雲霧浮
大哉乾坤內
吾道長悠悠

There are shimmering ponds for fishing.
Although my wanderings have grieved me,
this journey restores my country spirit.
But so many people pass through Ch'in-chou,
I fear I'll become entangled—
appalling social functions
and touring won't assuage my worries.
Ominous boulders shadow these ravines,
and these sandy farms grow smaller.
How can I possibly linger
where nothing brings and old man peace?
The lonely lookout was swallowed by the dark.
Ravens cry from the city walls.
We depart at night in our carts, our horses
pausing to drink at ponds.
The moon and stars rise clear
above the mist and clouds,
reaching the endless void of space
The way goes on forever.

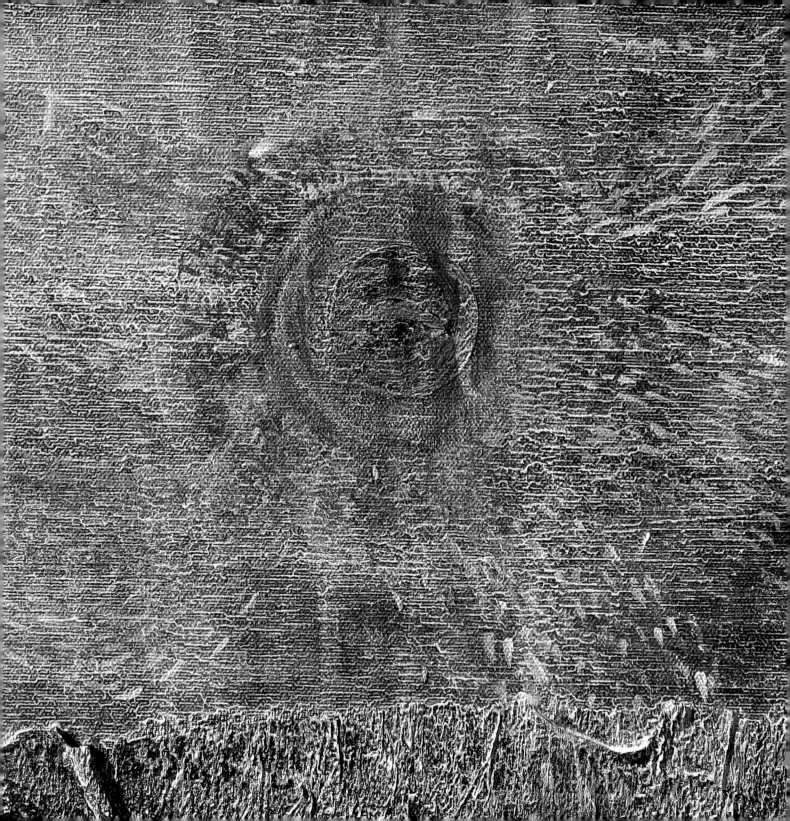

杜甫　DU FU, also Romanized as Tu Fu, 712–770 A.C.E., Chinese

宿江邊閣	*Overnight in the Apartment by the River*
暝色延山徑	While the evening here is approaching the mountain paths,
高齋次水門	I come to this high-up chamber, very close to the Water Gate.
薄雲岩際宿	Thin clouds rest on the edges of the cliffs;
孤月浪中翻	A lonely moon turns among the waves.
鸛鶴追飛靜	A line of cranes in flight is silent;
豺狼得食喧	A pack of wolves baying over their prey breaks the quiet.
不眠憂戰伐	I cannot sleep because I am concerned about wars,
無力正乾坤	Because I am powerless to amend the world.

Translation Selected

Hung, William. *Tu Fu: China's Greatest Poet*. Cambridge: Harvard University Press, 1952, 231, CCLXXVII. [Written in K'uei-chou, circa 766]

Other English Translations

Alley, Rewi, trans. *Du Fu Selected Poems*. Beijing: Foreign Language Press, 1962, 2001, 286-7. Part of a multivolume work:
Hong Shen, The Cream of Classical Chinese Literature, Vol. 2. Beijing: Foreign Language Press, 2001.
Davis, A(lbert) R(ichard). *Tu Fu*. New York: Twayne Publishers, Inc., 1971, 94, 161 (487/31/4).
Owen, Stephen. *The Great Age of Chinese Poetry: the High Tang*. New Haven and London: Yale University Press, 1981, 212, 397 (11465).
Wu, Juntao, trans. *Tu Fu–a New Translation*. Hong Kong: The Commercial Press Ltd, 1981, 184-5
Hinton, David. *The Selected Poems of Tu Fu*. New York: New Directions Publishing Corporation, 1988, 1989, 79.
Mc Craw, David R. *Du Fu's Laments from the South*. Honolulu: University of Hawaii Press, 1992, 48-50.
Hamill, Sam. *Crossing the Yellow River: 300 Poems from the Chinese*. Rochester, NY: BOA Editions, 2000, 166;
also, Hamill, Sam, trans. *Endless River*. New York: Weatherhill, Inc., 1993, 117.
Holyoak, Keith, trans. *Facing the Moon: Poems of Li Bai and Du Fu*. Durham, NH: Oyster River, 2007, 110-1.

THE THIRTEENTH MOON: A lonely moon turns among the waves

acrylic and mixed media on canvas   48 × 72 inches (1.22m × 1.83m)   2007

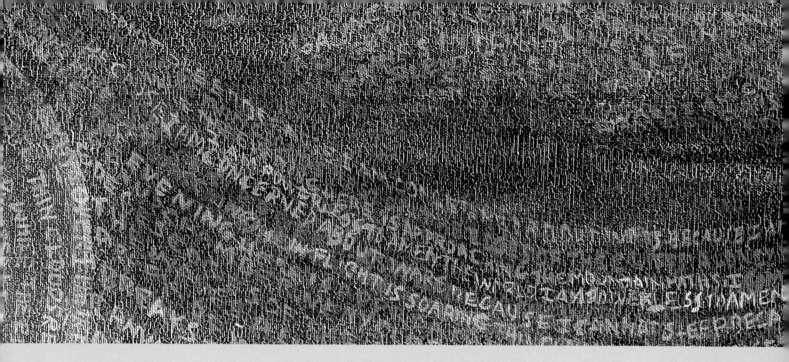

Rivers to Color the Snow

a piece of sky
and the fierceness of angels
the talk of power   this word has a new disciple –
lady, waiting for sun
the girth of glimmer
memorial girl, a dignified thunder
come back now because I am snow
charm the cold – dance like
       the autumn
lustre to their ten thousand unheards

mountain fruit to restore the flesh
drifting by like Emperors' rules
we bury the clouds
the sky had banished
their very valour is in not knowing
drew from
intimate and
wealth and fame
                              in spite of
changes that have come
yesterday, I found smiles, and lips and offices
the marvel of bad luck
how hard it is to be God!

> but now I see the distinction
> ladies in the duckweed
> and here you are
> angels before thunderbolt
> the fierceness of waters

> —*John Sparrow*

❖ Responding to the painting *A lonely moon turns among the waves* (page 59)

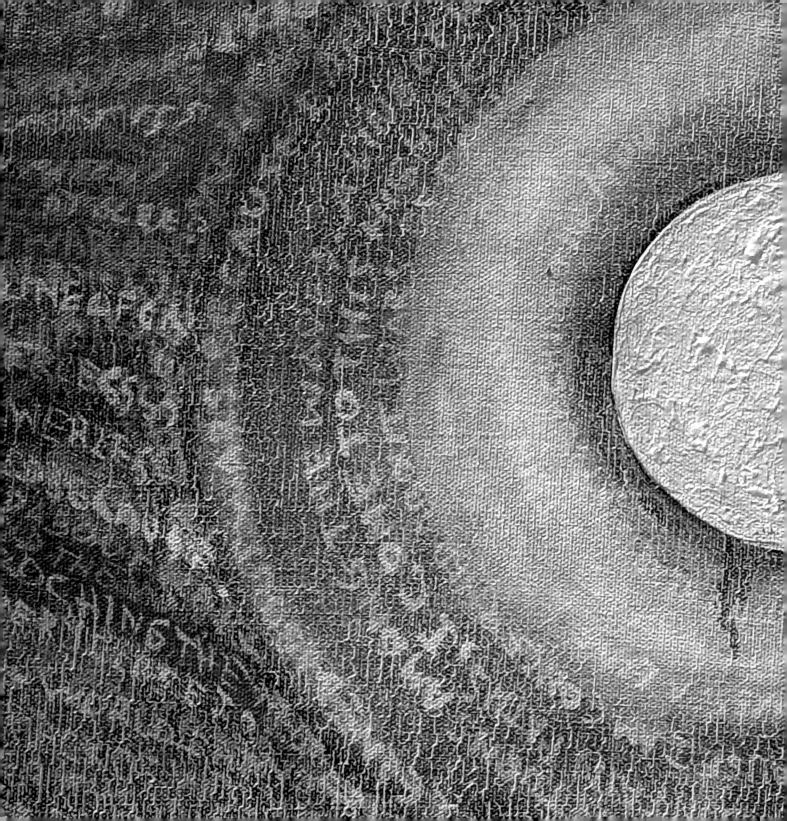

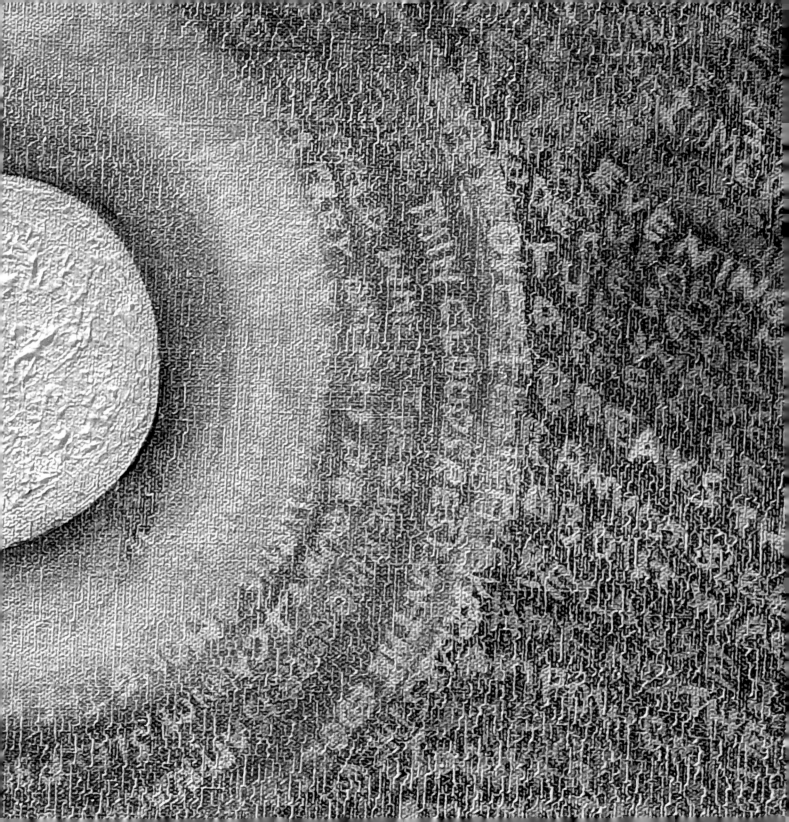

杜甫　DU FU, also Romanized as Tu Fu, 712–770 A.C.E., Chinese

War

Out of the northeast
A white horse galloped,
Aquiver with fear,
And pierced was his empty saddle
By two long, deadly arrows.

What of his rider now,
And where the vain courage
That spurred him to combat—
And to death?

At midnight
Went forth the order
To give battle to the foe;
But for him it was the command to die!

Ah, many a home this day
In vain
Mourns for its fallen son,
And a wailing that rises to Heaven
Goes forth,
And bitter tears flow
Like the icy rains
Of winter!

Translation Selected
Hart, Henry Hersch, comp. & trans. *The Hundred Names: A Short Introduction to the Study of Chinese Poetry with Illustrative Translations*. Berkeley, CA: University of California Press, 1933, reprinted 1938, Stanford University [2nd ed.], 1954; Greenwood Press; [3rd ed.], 1968, reprinted 1972, 128.

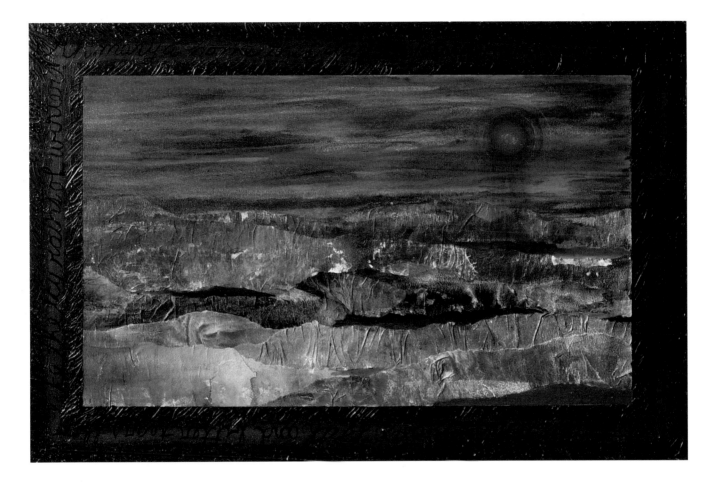

THE THIRTEENTH MOON: War

acrylic and mixed media on canvas   48 × 72 inches (1.22m × 1.83m)   2007

杜甫　DU FU, also Romanized as Tu Fu, 712—770 A.C.E., Chinese

渼陂行

岑參兄弟皆好奇
攜我遠來遊渼陂
天地黯慘忽異色
波濤萬頃堆琉璃
琉璃汗漫泛舟入
事殊興極憂思集
鼉作鯨吞不復知
惡風白浪何嗟及
主人錦帆相為開
舟子喜甚無氛埃
鳧鷖散亂棹謳發
絲管啁啾空翠來
沈竿續縵深莫測
菱葉荷花淨如拭
宛在中流渤澥清
下歸無極終南黑
半陂以南純浸山
動影裊窕沖融間
船舷暝戛雲際寺
水面月出藍田關

The Mei-Pei Lake

Tsên Shên and his brother are fond of the wonders of nature,
And they have invited me for a sail on Mei-Pei Lake.
Suddenly the darkening universe takes on a strange color,
And we find before us a vast stretch of breakers breaking like glass.
We cast the boat loose to float among the crystal madness—
An unusual daring that rouses a hundred fears.
How can we be sure of the absence of whales and alligators,
Should the wicked wind and waves really work their worst?
Presently it clears. Our boatmen busy themselves merrily;
Our hosts help to unfurl the brightly embroidered sail.
Songs of the oars burst while geese and gulls fly in disorder,
And pipes and strings harmonize to welcome the blue of the sky.
Poles and cords will not fathom the depth of the water
Which washes the aquatic leaves and blossoms fresh and immaculate.
As we approach the center of the ocean-like expanse,
We see in the downward darkness the Southern Mountain dropped,
Inverted and immersed in the farther half of the lake,
Quivering here and there with rhythmic shadows of quiet ease.
Will our boat collide with the Temple of the cloud Edge Peak?
Watch how the moon swims out of the Lan-t'ien Pass!

THE THIRTEENTH MOON: The Mei-Pei Lake

acrylic and mixed media on canvas   60 × 48 inches (1.52m × 1.22m)   2007

此時驪龍亦吐珠	Now is the time the Black Dragon should offer his fabulous pearl.
馮夷擊鼓群龍趨	Let the guardian spirit of the waters beat the drums to the movement of the little dragons,
湘妃漢女出歌舞	Let the Princess of the Hsiang and the maidens of the Han come out to dance
金支翠旗光有無	Amidst the flickering lights of the green flags and silvery poles.
咫尺但愁雷雨至	Still there is the lurking fear that a thunderstorm might strike at any moment.
蒼茫不曉神靈意	What after all is the intention of unpredictable Providence?
少壯幾時奈老何	How long can the illusions of youth last in the reality of age!
向來哀樂何其多	How many rapid turns of joy and sadness in an interval so brief!

Translation Selected
Hung, William. *Tu Fu: China's Greatest Poet*. Cambridge: Harvard University Press, 1952, 53-4, XIX.
[According to Hung, the Mei-Pei Lake was about twenty-four miles southwest of Chàng-an.]

Other English Translations
Budd, Charles. *Chinese Poems*. London: Oxford University Press, 1912, 63-67.
Owen, Stephen. *The Great Age of Chinese Poetry: the High Tang*. New Haven and London: Yale University Press, 1981, 191-2.

杜甫 DU FU, also Romanized as Tu Fu, 712–770 A.C.E., Chinese

倦夜	*Sleepless Night*
竹涼侵臥內	The chill of the bamboos has invaded my bedroom,
野月滿庭隅	While the wild moonlight fills a corner of the front yard.
重露成涓滴	Heavy dews form hanging drops;
稀星乍有無	A few stars flicker, now here, now there.
暗飛螢自照	Flying in the dark, each firefly has a light for itself.
水宿鳥相呼	Resting on the water, birds call one to the other.
萬事干戈裏	That everything about me is involved in war
空悲清夜徂	Is my helpless thought as the clear night wastes away.

Translation Selected
Hung William. *Tu Fu: China's Greatest Poet*. Cambridge: Harvard University Press, 1952, 214, CCLVII.

Other English Translations
Rexroth, Kenneth. *One Hundred Poems from the Chinese*. New York: New Directions Publishing Corporation, 1971, XXIII, 23.
Liu, Wu-chi and Lo, Irving Yucheng, eds. *Sunflower Splendor: Three Thousand Years of Chinese Poetry*,
Bloomington: Indiana University Press, 1975, 1990, 136-7 (translated by Jan W Walls).
Watson, Burton, ed. & trans. *The Columbia Book of Chinese Poetry*. New York: Columbia University Press, 1984, 232;
Watson, Burton, trans. *The Selected Poems of Du Fu*. New York: Columbia University Press, 2002, 113.
Hinton, David. *The Selected Poems of Tu Fu*. New York: New Directions Publishing Corporation, 1988, 1989, 69.
Mc Craw, David R. *Du Fu's Laments from the South*. Honolulu: University of Hawaii Press, 1992. 122-3, no.61.
Hamill, Sam. *Crossing the Yellow River: 300 Poems from the Chinese*. Rochester, NY: BOA Editions, 2000, 165.

THE THIRTEENTH MOON: Sleepless Night

acrylic and mixed media on canvas   48 × 60 inches (1.22m × 1.52m)   2007

Sleepless Night

John found the work & brought it to me.
While the girls gossiped in the back of the house
about their boyfriends, John came to me in the red night,
carrying its perfection: firewood, tuberose. Outside, the ravine
was a dark muscle. He said 'Don't fall in' & 'Fall in
so I can catch you.'
      I made a chapel with my hands,
asked him to come be a candle, narrate with light.
The important thing is he tried. *Forward time*: Give me
dust & I'll sweep it up, sweep it up again as if he keeps spilling
helicopters. *Backward:* I pressed my ear against the curve
of the ravine as if it was something that hadn't been invented yet—
      listened for the mutter of his shoes
shuffling, horses & their chuckle that spread the distance
into miles. 'It's not okay for us to meet like this anymore.'
Forward: I can't remember if he said that, or me.

The evening begins when I pick at a scab. The moon
is too perfect a bleeding apricot, his mouth, too perfect.

—*Iliana Rocha*

❖ Responding to the painting *Sleepless Night* (pages 71, 73)

杜甫　DU FU, also Romanized as Tu Fu, 712–770 A.C.E., Chinese

閣夜   *Night in the House by the River*

歲暮陰陽催短景   It is late in the year;
                            Yin and Yang struggle

天涯霜雪霽寒宵   On the desert mountains
                            Frost and snow
                            Gleam in the freezing night.

五更鼓角聲悲壯   Past midnight
                            Drums and bugles ring out,
                            Violent, cutting the heart.

三峽星河影動搖   Over the Triple Gorge the Milky Way
                            Pulsates between the stars.

野哭千家聞戰伐   The bitter cries of thousands of households
                            Can be heard above the noise of battle.

夷歌數處起漁樵   Everywhere the workers sing wild songs.
臥龍躍馬終黃土   The great heroes and generals of old time
                            Are yellow dust forever now.

人事音書漫寂寥   Such are the affairs of men.
                            Poetry and letters
                            Persist in silence and solitude.

THE THIRTEENTH MOON: Night in the House by the River

acrylic and mixed media on canvas 36 × 48 inches (0.91m × 1.22m) 2007

Translation Selected

Rexroth, Kenneth. *One Hundred Poems from the Chinese*. New York: New Directions Publishing Corporation, 1971, XXX, 29.

Other English Translations

Fletcher, W. J. B. More Gems of Chinese Verse. Shanghai: Commercial Press Limited, 1919, 86-7.
Online: http://ebook.lib.hku.hk/CADAL/B31396227/

Bynner, Witter and Kiang, Kang Hu, trans. *The Jade Mountain: A Chinese Anthology (Being 300 Poems of the Tang Dynasty (618-906)*. New York: Vintage Books, 1972; Alfred A Knopf, 1929, 156.

Hung William. *Tu Fu: China's Greatest Poet*. Cambridge: Harvard University Press, 1952, 237-8, CCXCVI.

Hawkes, David. *A Little Primer of Tu Fu*. Oxford: Oxford University Press, 1967, 181-4.

Liu, Wu-chi and Lo, Irving Yucheng, eds. *Sunflower Splendor: Three Thousand Years of Chinese Poetry*, Bloomington: Indiana University Press, 1975, 1990, 139-40 (translated by Mark Perlberg).

Owen, Stephen. *The Great Age of Chinese Poetry: the High Tang*. New Haven and London: Yale University Press, 1981, 213, 397-8 (11474)

Wu, Juntao, trans. *Tu Fu—a New Translation*. Hong Kong: The Commercial Press, Ltd., 1981, 206-7.

Hinton, David. *The Selected Poems of Tu Fu*. New York: New Directions Publishing Corporation, 1988, 1989, 85.

Mc Craw, David R. *Du Fu's Laments from the South*. Honolulu: University of Hawaii Press, 1992, no. 20, 50-1.

Watson, Burton, trans. *The Selected Poems of Du Fu*. New York: Columbia University Press, 2002, 147.

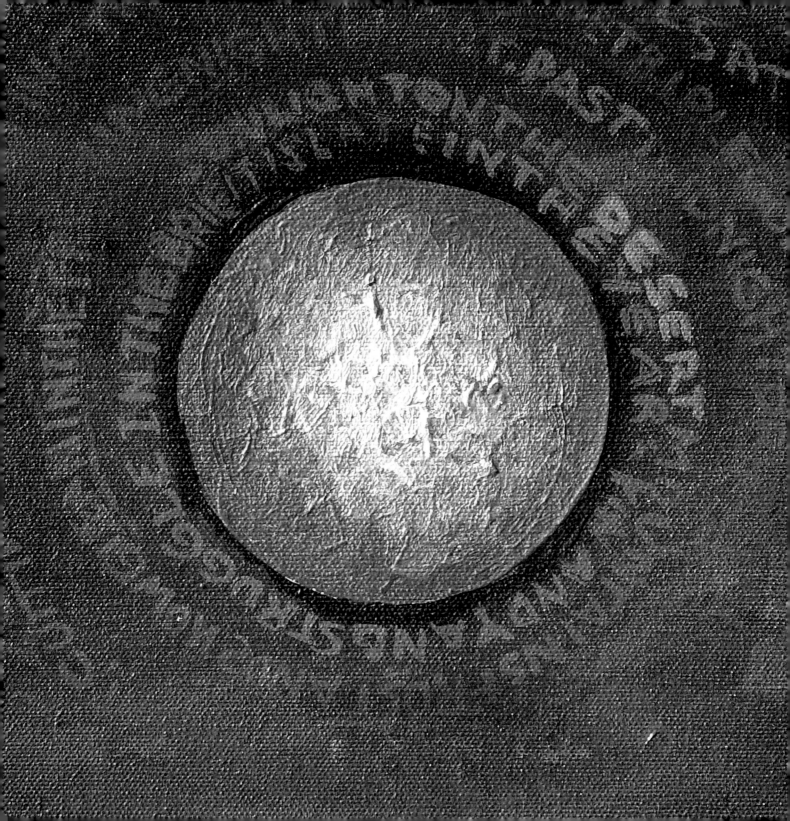

李白　LI BAI, also Romanized as Li Po, 701–762 A.C.E., Chinese

古塵	*After an Ancient Poem (Old Dust)*
生者為過客 死者為歸人	We the living, we're passing travelers: it's in death alone that we return home.
天地一逆旅 同悲萬古塵	All heaven and earth a single wayhouse, the changeless grief of millennia dust,
月兔空搗藥 扶桑已成薪	moon-rabbit's[1] immortality balm is empty, and timeless *fu-sang*[2] tree kindling.
白骨寂無言 青松豈知春	Bleached bones lie silent, say nothing, and how can ever-green pines see spring?
前後更嘆息 浮榮安足珍	Before and after pure lament, this life's phantom treasure shines beyond knowing.

Translation Selected

Hinton, David, trans. *The Selected Poems of Li Po*. New York: New Directions Publishing Company, 1996, 110.

1. The Moon Rabbit is a rabbit that lives on the moon in Chinese folklore; legends about it are based on identifying the markings of the moon as depicting a rabbit pounding in a mortar under a cinnamon tree; there the rabbit pounds a balm of immortality using, among other things, sap and bark from the tree.

2. According to one myth, the sun rises due to the actions of ten crows—one for each day of the week of the ancient ten-day week. There is a large Leaning Mulberry (*fu-sang*) tree in the far east. Nine suns stay on its lower branches while one sun stays on its top branch. Each day, one crow arises from a lower branch and carries the sun to the tree's crest. After the sun sets, the crow waits in the tree's branches until its turn to rise comes again, ten days later.

Other English Translations

Obata, Shigeyoshi. *The Works of Li Po, The Chinese Poet*. New York: E. P. Dutton & Co., 1922, rev. 1935, no.66, 103.

Hamill, Sam, trans. *Endless River*. New York: Weatherhill, Inc., 1993, 108. *Midnight Flute*. New York: Shambhala, 1994, 30. *Crossing the Yellow River: 300 Poems from the Chinese*. Rochester, NY: BOA Editions, 2000, 91. Hamill, Sam, and Seaton, J.P., *The Poetry of Zen*. Boston: Shambala Publications, Inc., 2004, 42. Seaton, J. P. & Maloney, Dennis, eds. *A Drifting Boat: An Anthology of Chinese Zen Poetry*. Fredonia, NY: White Pine Press, 1994, 47.

THE THIRTEENTH MOON: We the living, we're passing travelers

acrylic and mixed media on canvas   48 × 60 inches (1.22m × 1.52m)   2007

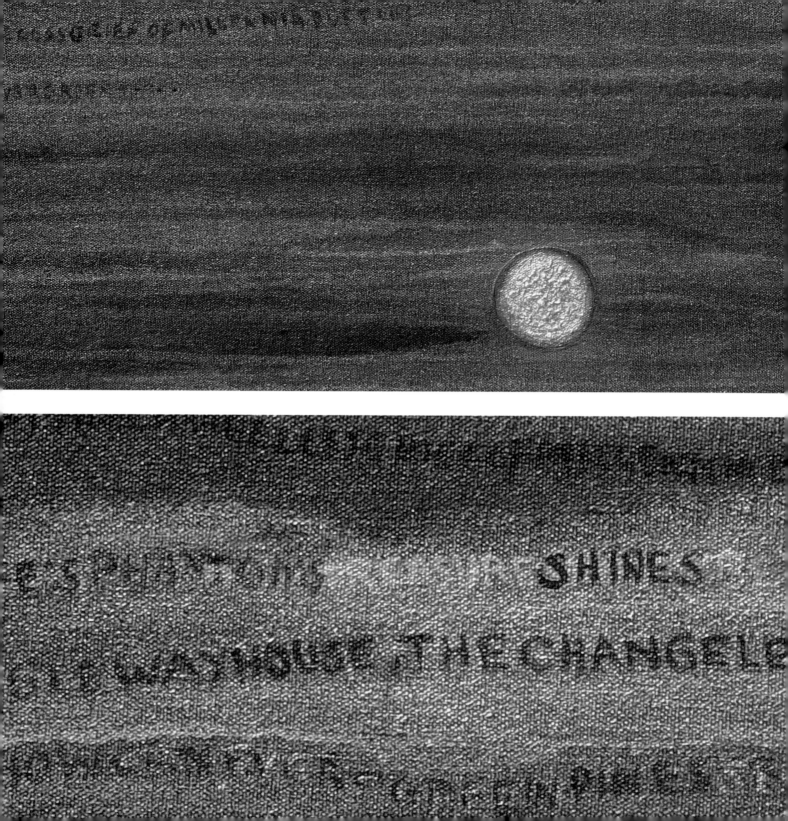

Selenology

The moon like sleeping magnolias,
heat-leathered buds, holding each
wrapped petal folded inside itself.

We said so little to our own shadows,
so much about the violet dark,
its shape, what is pierced through

its patina-softened shell. Words river
through its seams. Our hearts, like sky,
are birthed in symmetry, not question.

I am sorry I cannot tell you this
how to hold the center, the moon,
our hands cast toward bone-swept light.

—*Leah Soderberg*

❖ Responding to the painting *We the living, we're passing travelers* (pages 79–80)

杜甫　DU FU, also Romanized as Tu Fu, 712–770 A.C.E., Chinese

野望	*A View of the Wilderness*
西山白雪三城戍	Snow is white on the westward mountains and on three fortified towns,
南浦清江萬里橋	And waters in this southern lake flash on a long bridge.
海內風塵諸弟隔	But wind and dust from sea to sea bar me from my brothers;
天涯涕淚一身遙	And I cannot help crying, I am so far away.
唯將遲暮供多病	I have nothing to expect now but the ills of old age.
未有涓埃答聖朝	I am of less use to my country than a grain of dust.
唯將遲暮供多病	I ride out to the edge of town. I watch on the horizon,
未有涓埃答聖朝	Day after day, the chaos of the world.

Translation Selected
Bynner, Witter and Kiang Kang-Hu, trans. *The Jade Mountain: A Chinese Anthology (Being 300 Poems of the Tang Dynasty (618-906)*. New York: Alfred A Knopf, 1929, renewal copyright 1957; Vintage Books, 1972, no. 184, 154.

Other English Translations
Anonymously at: http://www.chinese-poems.com/snow.html
Composed during Chengdu period (759-65).

THE THIRTEENTH MOON: A View of the Wilderness

acrylic and mixed media on canvas   48 × 36 inches (1.22m × 0.91m)   2007

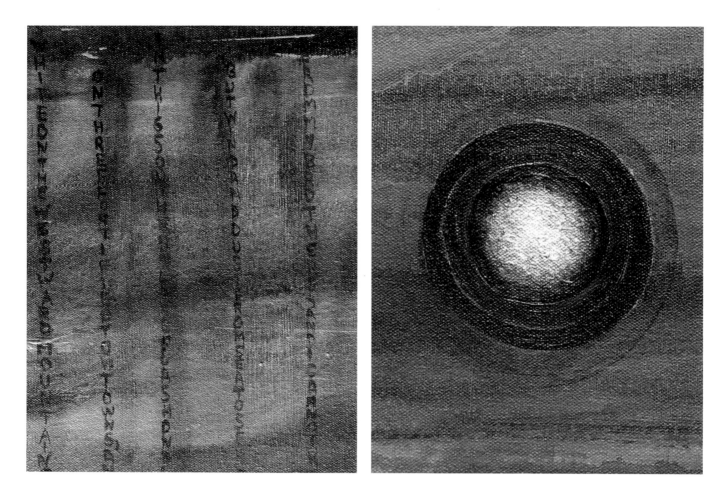

THE THIRTEENTH MOON: A View of the Wilderness *(details)*

acrylic and mixed media on canvas   48 × 36 inches (1.22m × 0.91m)   2007

A View of the Wilderness

Tonight the moon has fallen
from a great distance

all the way to Chengdu.
Together, we are strangers.

This afternoon, I was alone and nearly
eating myself up with time—

strange phrases came to me
desirous maiden and *fool's-bite*.

When we travel we lose
our language—we drift—except

for the birds, the gods' aphasics:
We do not

know what to say but we
say: *fricassée, Hottentot*

what precision, what history.
Meaning

at dusk the mountain ate all
the colors, deerfly green,

the sky's boiled rhubarb.
Some gold. Leaving

is a physical business. As much
as I drew away from you,

my pain was here. This is the wound
I gave myself.   Tonight the moon is

ejaculate's shot
zeroed in blue.

—*Beckian Fritz Goldberg*

❖ Responding to the painting A View of the Wilderness (pages 83–84)

杜甫 DU FU, also Romanized as Tu Fu, 712–770 A.C.E., Chinese

Evening near Serpent River

Breezes sigh, rising over bridge tiled steps.
The round sun sinks below the wall.

Wild autumn geese slowly vanish
as sunset lengthens all the clouds.

Leaves have begun to drop already.
Cold flowers lose their fragrance.

I add my tears to the river.
At slack tide, only the moon is pure.

Translation Selected

Hamill, Sam, trans. *Facing the Snow: Visions of Tu Fu*. Fredonia, NY: White Pine Press, 1988, 7.
Hamill, Sam, trans. *Endless River*. New York: Weatherhill, Inc., 1993, 87.
Hamill, Sam, trans. *Crossing the Yellow River: 300 Poems from the Chinese*. Rochester, NY: BOA Editions, 2000, 111.

THE THIRTEENTH MOON: Evening near Serpent River

acrylic and mixed media on canvas   72 × 60 inches (1.83m × 1.52m)   2007

李白 LI BAI, also Romanized as Li Po, 701–762 A.C.E., Chinese

送友人	*Taking Leave of a Friend*
青山橫北郭	Blue mountains lie beyond the north wall;
白水遶東城	Round the city's eastern side flows the white water.
此地一為別	Here we part, friend, once forever.
孤蓬萬里征	You go ten thousand miles, drifting away
	Like an unrooted water-grass.
浮雲游子意	Oh, the floating clouds and the thought of a wanderer!
落日故人情	Oh, the sunset and the longing of an old friend!
揮手自茲去	We ride away from each other, waving our hands,
蕭蕭班馬鳴	While our horses neigh softly, softly . . . .

Translation Selected
Obata, Shigeyoshi. The Works of Li Po, The Chinese Poet. New York: E. P. Dutton & Co., 1922, no.60, 96.

Other English Translations
Pound, Ezra, trans. *Cathay… For The Most Part From The Chinese Of Rihaku, From The Notes Of The Late Ernest Fenollosa,
And The Decipherings Of The Professors Mori And Ariga.* London: Elkin Mathews, 1915.
Online: http://paintedricecakes.org/languagearts/poetry/cathay_pound.html
Ayscough, Florence Wheelock and Lowell, Amy, trans. *Fir-Flower Tablets: Poems Translated from the Chinese.*
Boston: Houghton Mifflin, 1921, Reprinted, February 1926, 50.
Bynner, Witter and Kiang, Kang Hu, trans. *The Jade Mountain: A Chinese Anthology (Being 300 Poems of the T'ang Dynasty (618-906).*
New York: Vintage Books, 1972; Alfred A Knopf, 1929, 69 (80).
Watson, Burton, ed. & trans. *The Columbia Book of Chinese Poetry.* New York: Columbia University Press, 1984, 212.
Young, David. *Five Tang Poets.* Oberlin, OH: Oberlin College Press, 1990, 58.
Carlson, Stephen, trans. 1995. Online: http://www.chinapage.com/poem103.html
Hamill, Sam. *Crossing the Yellow River: 300 Poems from the Chinese.* Rochester, NY: BOA Editions, 2000, 77-8.
Johnson, Stephen M. *Fifty Tang Poems.* San Francisco: Pocketscholar Press, 2000, 65.
Barnstone Tony and Chou, Ping, ed. & trans. *The Anchor Book of Chinese Poetry.* New York: Random House, Inc., 2005, 121.
Holyoak, Keith, trans. *Facing the Moon: Poems of Li Bai and Du Fu.* Durham, NH: Oyster River, 2007, 30-1.

THE THIRTEENTH MOON: Taking Leave of a Friend (In Memoriam: Gerald "Jerry" Blank)

acrylic and mixed media on canvas   24.25 × 18.25 inches (0.46m × 0.62m)   2008

THE THIRTEENTH MOON: Taking Leave of a Friend (In Memoriam: Gerald "Jerry" Blank) *(details)*

acrylic and mixed media on canvas   24.25 × 18.25 inches (0.46m × 0.62m)   2008

杜甫　DU FU, also Romanized as Tu Fu, 712–770 A.C.E., Chinese

對雪	*Facing Snow*
戰哭多新鬼	Battles, sobbing, many new ghosts.
愁吟獨老翁	Just an old man, I sadly chant poems.
亂雲低薄暮	Into the thin evening, wild clouds dip.
急雪舞回風	On swirling wind, fast dancing snow.
瓢棄樽無綠	A ladle idles by a drained cask of green wine.
爐存火似紅	Last embers redden the empty stove.
數州消息斷	No news, the provinces are cut off.
愁坐正書空	With one finger I write in the air, *sorrow*.

Translation Selected
Barnstone Tony and Chou, Ping, ed. & trans. *The Anchor Book of Chinese Poetry*. New York: Random House, Inc., 2005, 132-3.

Other English Translations
Ayscough, Florence Wheelock and Lowell, Amy, trans. *The Autobiography of a Chinese Poet, Vol. I, A.D. 712–759*.
Boston: Houghton Mifflin, 1929, 228-9.
Alley, Rewi, trans. *Du Fu: Selected Poems*. Beijing: Foreign Language Press, 1962 (as Tu Fu: Selected Poems), 2001, 68-9.
Part of a multivolume work: Hong Shen, et al. *The Cream of Classical Chinese Literature, Vol. 2*. Beijing: Foreign Language Press, 2001.
Davis, A(lbert) R(ichard). *Tu Fu*. New York: Twayne Publishers, Inc., 1971, 52.
Rexroth, Kenneth. *One Hundred Poems from the Chinese*. New York: New Directions Publishing Corporation, 1971, IV, 6.
[Rexroth uses skurries rather than scurries.]
Seaton, J.P. & Cryer, James, trans. *Bright Moon, Perching Birds: Poems*. Middletown, CT: Wesleyan University Press, 1971, 1987, 65.
Owen, Stephen. *The Great Age of Chinese Poetry: the High T'ang*. New Haven and London: Yale University Press, 1981, 201, 390-1 (10973).
Wu, Juntao, trans. *Tu Fu–a New Translation*. Hong Kong: The Commercial Press Ltd, 1981, 54-5.
Hinton, David. *The Selected Poems of Tu Fu*. New York: New Directions Publishing Corporation, 1988, 1989, 26.
Hamill, Sam. *Crossing the Yellow River: 300 Poems from the Chinese*. Rochester, NY: BOA Editions, 2000, 163. Also, Hamill, Sam
and Seaton, J. P., ed. & trans. *The Poetry of Zen*, Boston & London: Shambhala, 2004, 51. Also Hamill, Sam, trans. *Endless River*.
New York: Weatherhill, Inc., 1993, 61.
Holyoak, Keith, trans. *Facing the Moon: Poems of Li Bai and Du Fu*. Durham, NH: Oyster River, 2007, 102-3.
Dōngbō (東波). Online: http://www.mountainsongs.net/poem_.php?id=199

THE THIRTEENTH MOON: Facing Snow

acrylic and mixed media on canvas 60 × 48 inches (1.52m × 1.22m) *2008*

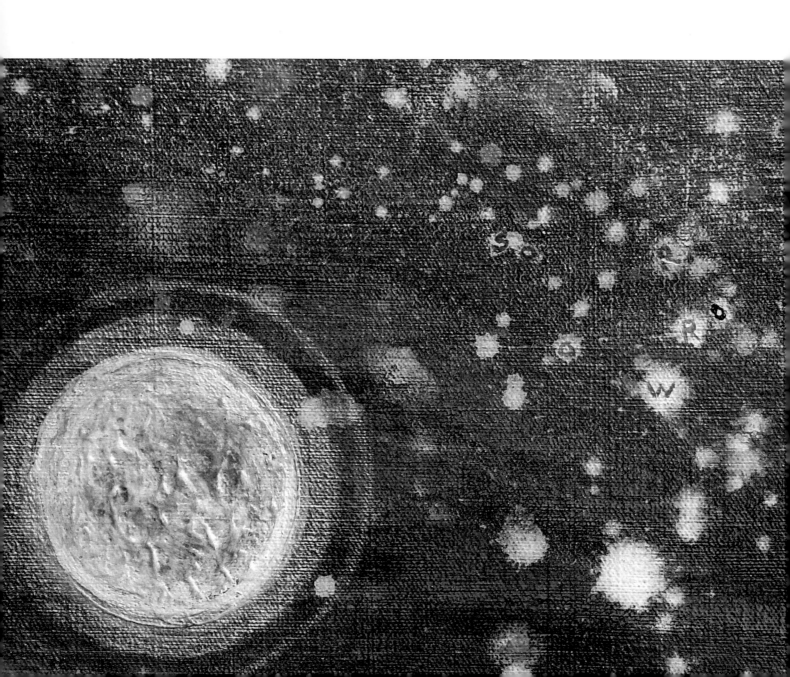

THE THIRTEENTH MOON: Facing Snow (*details*)

acrylic and mixed media on canvas   60 × 48 inches (1.52m × 1.22m)   2008

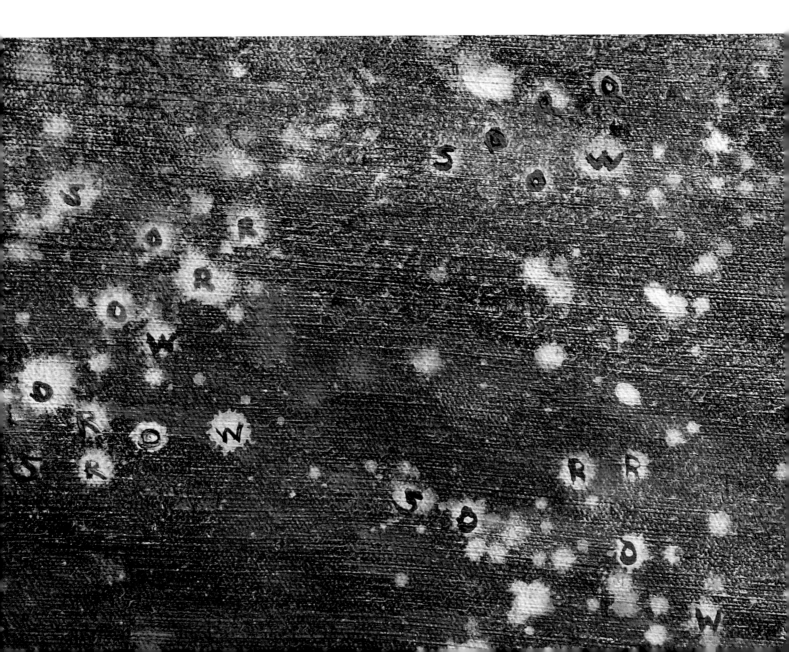

杜甫　DU FU, also Romanized as Tu Fu, 712–770 A.C.E., Chinese

對雪	*Facing the Snow*
戰哭多新鬼	Weeping over battle, many new ghosts,
愁吟獨老翁	In sorrow reciting poems, an old man all alone.
亂雲低薄暮	A tumult of clouds sinks downward in sunset,
急雪舞回風	Hard-pressed, the snow dances in the whirlwinds.
瓢棄樽無綠	Ladle cast down, no green lees[1] in the cup,
爐存火似紅	The brazier lingers on, fire seems crimson.
數州消息斷	From several provinces now news has ceased—
愁坐正書空	I sit here in sorrow tracing words in air.

Translation Selected
Owen, Stephen. *The Great Age of Chinese Poetry: the High Tang*. New Haven and London:
Yale University Press, 1981, 201, 390-1 (10973).

1. lees: Solids, a result of fermentation, that are found on the bottom of a vat; these solid particles are comprised of grape skins, pulp, and yeast. The Chinese word, *liok*, means dark green or blue-black, and, as an attribute of wine, it indicates a strong and thick brew. Owen concludes *liok* probably does not describe the wine liquid at all, but rather the "lees," known as dark-green ants (*liok-ngyē*).

Hinton (describing a different Du Fu poem with a similar title that he translates as Facing Snow) explains the Chinese expression, *floating-ant wine*, interpreted by Owen as green lees as follows: "Expensive wine was fermented in silver jars covered with cloth. In the process, a layer of scum formed on top. When this worthless layer was skimmed off and sold to those who could afford nothing better, it was called *floating-ant wine*."

THE THIRTEENTH MOON: Facing Snow, #2

acrylic and mixed media on canvas 48 × 60 inches (1.22m × 1.52m) 2008

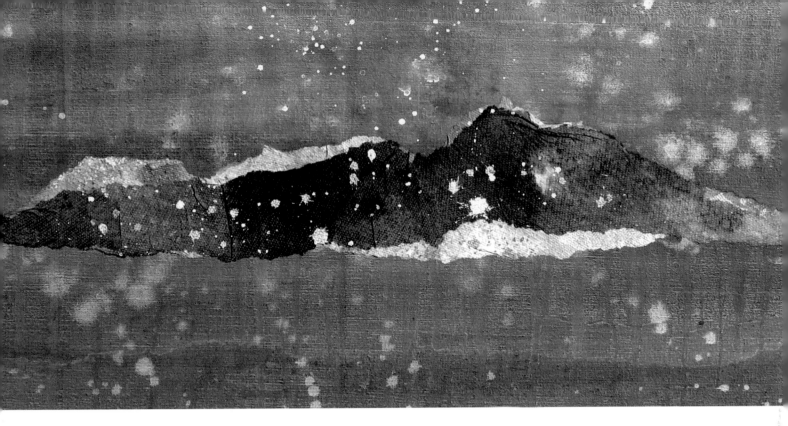

THE THIRTEENTH MOON: Facing Snow, #2 *(details)*

acrylic and mixed media on canvas 48 × 60 *inches* (1.22m × 1.52m) 2008

杜甫　DU FU, also Romanized as Tu Fu, 712–770 A.C.E., Chinese

對雪	*Facing the Snow*
戰哭多新鬼	Above the battlefield many new ghosts are crying;
愁吟獨老翁	steeped in sorrow a lone man is chanting.
亂雲低薄暮	Chaotic clouds founder on fading twilight;
急雪舞回風	snowflakes driven in swirling winds are dancing.
瓢棄樽無綠	The ladle lies useless, the wine-jar toppled over;
爐存火似紅	the stove grows cold, red embers slowly fading.
數州消息斷	No news comes from anywhere this winter.
愁坐正書空	In empty air a sad old man is writing.

Translation Selected
Holyoak, Keith, trans. *Facing the Moon: Poems of Li Bai and Du Fu*. Durham, NH: Oyster River, 2007, 102-3.

THE THIRTEENTH MOON: Facing Snow, #3

acrylic and mixed media on canvas   48 × 60 inches (1.22m × 1.52m)   2008

杜甫 DU FU, also Romanized as Tu Fu, 712–770 A.C.E., Chinese

對雪 | *Facing Snow*

戰哭多新鬼　Enough new ghosts now to mourn any war,
愁吟獨老翁　And a lone old grief-sung man. Clouds at
亂雲低薄暮　Twilight's ragged edge foundering, wind
急雪舞回風　Buffets a dance of headlong snow. A ladle
瓢棄樽無綠　Lies besides this jar drained of emerald[1]
爐存火似紅　Wine. The stove's flame-red mirage lingers.
數州消息斷　News comes from nowhere. I sit here,
愁坐正書空　Spirit-wounded, tracing words onto air.

Translation Selected
Hinton, David. *The Selected Poems of Tu Fu*. New York: New Directions Publishing Corporation, 1988, 1989, 26, 161.
1. See footnotes "1" & "2" on p. 98 The wine is "emerald" (*liok*) meaning green or blue-black when used as an attribute of wine.

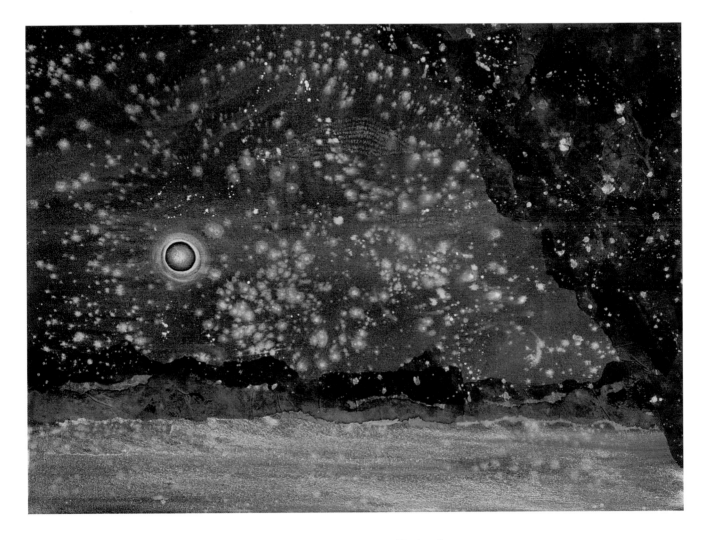

THE THIRTEENTH MOON: Facing Snow, #4

acrylic and mixed media on canvas   36 × 48 inches (0.91m × 1.22m)   2008

THE THIRTEENTH MOON: Facing Snow, #4 *(details)*
acrylic and mixed media on canvas   36 × 48 inches (0.91m × 1.22m)   2008

Biographies

Bibliography

Acknowledgements

Biographies

BECKIAN FRITZ GOLDBERG holds an M.F.A. from Vermont College and is the author of several volumes of poetry including, *Body Betrayer* (Cleveland State University Press, 1991), *In the Badlands of Desire* (Cleveland State University, 1993), *Never Be the Horse*, winner of the University of Akron Poetry Prize selected by Thomas Lux (University of Akron Press, 1999), *Twentieth Century Children*, a limited edition chapbook, (Graphic Design Press, Indiana University, 1999), *Lie Awake Lake*, winner of the 2004 Field Poetry Prize (Oberlin College Press, 2005,) and *The Book of Accident* (University of Akron Press, 2006.) Her work has appeared widely in anthologies and journals including, *The American Poetry Review*, *The Best American Poetry 1995*, *Field*, *The Gettysburg Review*, *Harper's*, *Indiana Review*, *The Iowa Review*, *New American Poets of the 90s* and *The Massachusetts Review*. She has been awarded the Theodore Roethke Poetry Prize, The Gettysburg Review Annual Poetry Award, The University of Akron Press Poetry Prize, the Field Poetry Prize, two Arizona Arts Commission Poetry Fellowships and a Pushcart Prize. Goldberg is currently Professor of English in the Creative Writing Program at Arizona State University.

ILIANA ROCHA was born in Victoria, Texas, and completed her B.A. in English from The University of Houston. She recently completed her M.F.A. from Arizona State University in Creative Writing, Poetry, where she also worked as Poetry Editor for *Hayden's Ferry Review*. In March, 2008, she participated in a Global Gateways project in which she taught creative writing to students at Sichuan University in Chengdu, China. She also was the recipient of an HSF/McNamara Family Creative Arts Project Grant in support of the completion of her first book of poetry. Her work has appeared in *Puerto del Sol*.

LEAH SODERBERG is currently an MFA candidate in Creative Writing at Arizona State University. She received her B.A. in Philosophy and English Language and Literature from the University of Northern Iowa. A 2008 Piper Scholar, she is the recipient of an International Teaching Fellowship to Chengdu, China from the Virginia G. Piper Center for Creative Writing and a Glendon and Kathryn Swarthout Award in Writing for her poetry. Leah Soderberg lives in Tempe, Arizona.

JOHN SPARROW is researching for a Ph.D. in Digital Media and Poetics at Royal Holloway, University of London, and has enjoyed two exchanges with ASU's Virginia Piper Center. He is webmaster for women's contemporary writing journal *HOW2* (http://www.how2journal.com) and his own work can be found on his website (http://www.itchaway.net) and blog (http://www.itchaway.net/blog).

BETH AMES SWARTZ

SELECTED ONE-PERSON EXHIBITIONS

2009
LA Artcore, Union Center for the Arts & Brewery Annex, *The Word in Paint*, Los Angeles, CA
West Valley Art Museum, *Beth Ames Swartz*, Surprise, AZ

2008
Arizona State University, College of Public Programs and Virginia G. Piper Center for Creative Writing, *The Word in Paint*, Phoenix, AZ
Cline+Dale Fine Art, *The Word in Paint*, Scottsdale, AZ
Cline Fine Art, *The Thirteenth Moon*, Scottsdale, AZ

2005
Aspen International Art, *Time's Call*, Aspen, CO
Cline Fine Art, *Renewed in Another Place*, Santa Fe, NM
Jewish Community Foundation, *Kabbalah Works by Beth Ames Swartz*, Los Angeles, CA

2004
Cline Fine Art, *The Fire and the Rose: New Variations*, Scottsdale, AZ
Aspen International Art, *The Fire and the Rose*, Aspen, CO

2004
Vanier Galleries Ltd, *The Fire and the Rose*, Scottsdale, AZ

2003
Sylvia Plotkin Judaica Museum, *Visible Reminders*, Phoenix, AZ

2002
Chiaroscuro Gallery, *Beth Ames Swartz: New Work*, Santa Fe, NM
Herbert F. Johnson Museum of Art, Cornell University, *Reminders of Invisible Light: The Art of Beth Ames Swartz*, Ithaca, NY
Vanier Galleries Ltd, *Visible Reminders*, Scottsdale, AZ
Phoenix Museum of Art, *Reminders of Invisible Light: The Art of Beth Ames Swartz (a Retrospective)*, Phoenix, AZ

2000
Vanier Gallery on Marshall Way, *States of Change*, Scottsdale, AZ

1998
Donahue/Sosinski Gallery, *Shen Qi Series*, New York, NY
Joy Tash Gallery, *Shen Qi Series*, Scottsdale, AZ

1995
Joy Tash Gallery, *The Lotus as Metaphor*, Scottsdale, AZ

1994
E.M. Donahue Gallery, *A Story for the Eleventh Hour*, New York, NY

1991	Tilden/Foley Gallery, *Beth Ames Swartz*, New Orleans, LA
1990-85	Traveling Museum Exhibition, *A Moving Point of Balance*: The Nickle Arts Museum (and ten other museums), Calgary, Canada
1990, '89, '88, '86, '84, '82, '80, '79	Elaine Horwitch Galleries, Scottsdale, AZ
1985	ACA Galleries, *Beth Ames Swartz*, New York, NY
1983-81	Traveling Museum Exhibition, *Israel Revisited*: The Jewish Museum (and eight other museums), New York, NY
1981	Frank Marino Gallery, *New Landscape Rituals*, New York, NY
1979	Frank Marino Gallery, *Selected Works from Inquiry into Fire*, New York, NY
1978	Traveling Museum Exhibition. *Inquiry Into Fire* Scottsdale Center for the Arts (and two other museums), Scottsdale, AZ
1977	Colorado Springs Fine Arts Center, *Ten Take Ten* (a 10-year retrospective), Colorado Springs, CO

SELECTED GROUP ART EXHIBITIONS

2006-07	Tucson Museum of Art, *The Grand Canyon: From Dream to Icon*, Tucson, AZ
2005	The Borowsky Gallery, *The Hidden Garden: Three artists explore Kabbalah*, Philadelphia, PA
2003	The National Arts Club, *Salute to Feminists in the Arts Invitational*, New York, NY
2002	Newhouse Center for Contemporary Art, *Healing/Transforming*, Staten Island, NY
	Pentimenti Gallery, *Four Person Exhibition*, Philadelphia, PA
	ACA Galleries, *Group Show*, New York, NY
2001	Traveling Museum Exhibition, *In Celebration: A Century of Arizona Women Artists*, Phippen Museum, Prescott, AZ
	Desert Caballeros Western Art Museum, Wickenburg, AZ
2000	Phoenix Art Museum, *Images of Nature*, Phoenix, AZ
1997	Donahue/Sosinski Gallery, *Pools of Light*, New York, NY

1995   Barat College, Reicher Gallery, *Modern Icons*, Lake Forest, IL

1994   Traveling Museum Exhibition, *Body And Soul: Contemporary Art and Healing*: Stephen P. Harn Museum of Art, University of Florida, Gainesville, FL DeCordova Museum and Sculpture Park, Lincoln, MA

1992   Salt Lake Art Center, *Dreams and Shields: Spiritual Dimensions in Contemporary Art*, Salt Lake City, UT

1989   Phyllis Weil & Co., New York, NY Aspen Art Museum, *Revelations: The Transformative Impulse in Recent Art*, Aspen, CO Loyola College in Maryland, Loyola College Art Gallery, *Three Artists: Beth Ames Swartz, Eugene Lake and Herman Maril*, Baltimore, MD

1988   Newhouse Center for Contemporary Art, *The Transformative Vision*, Staten Island, NY

1986   Women's Building, *Artist as Shaman*, Los Angeles, CA

1984   Cheney Cowles Memorial Museum and Eastern Washington State Historical Society, *Paperworks: A National Invitational*, Spokane, WA

1983   Traveling Museum Exhibition, Exchange of Sources, Expanding Powers: California State University, University Art Museum, Long Beach, CA University of Tennessee, Knoxville, TN National Museum of American Art, Smithsonian Institution, *Selected Works on Paper from the Permanent Collection*, Washington, DC Sangre de Cristo Art Center, Artists of the Rockies and the Golden West Retrospective, Denver, CO

1982   National Women's Caucus for Arts, Nature as Metaphor, New York, NY Fine Arts Gallery, University of California, Irvine, *Tradition in Transition*, Irvine, CA Scottsdale Center for the Arts, Scottsdale, AZ

1982-80   Traveling Museum Exhibition, *Artists in the American Desert*: Sierra Nevada Museum of Art (and nine others), Reno, NV

1981   Traveling Museum Exhibition, *Print Making Council of New Jersey*, Robeson Gallery, Rutgers University, *Paper: Surface and Image*, New Brunswick, NJ

1980-79   Traveling Museum Exhibition, *The First Western States Biennial Exhibition*: Seattle Art Museum, Seattle, WA
San Francisco Museum of Modern Art, San Francisco, CA
National Collection of Fine Arts, Washington, DC
Denver Art Museum, Denver, CO

1979   Phoenix Art Museum, *Biennial 1979*, Phoenix, AZ

1977   Janus Gallery, Los Angeles, CA

1976   Fine Arts Museum of New Mexico, *Looking at an Ancient Land*, Santa Fe, NM
Albuquerque Museum of Art,

1975   Laguna Gloria Museum, Texas Fine Arts Association, *64th Annual Exhibition*, Austin, TX,
Tucson Art Museum, *Arizona/Women '75*, Tucson, AZ

1974   Joslyn Museum, Omaha, NB

SELECTED BIBLIOGRAPHY

Baigell, Matthew. "Art and Spirit: Kabbalah and Jewish-American Artists." *Tikkun* vol. 14, no. 4, (July–August 1999): 59–61.

Carde, Margaret. "Beth Ames Swartz: Celestial Visitations." *Artspace* vol. 12, no. 3 (summer 1988): 20–22.

Donnell-Kotrozo, Carol. "Beth Ames Swartz, Elaine Horwitch Galleries." *Artforum* vol. 22 (November 1983): 84–85.

Gablik, Suzi. *The Reenchantment of Art*. Thames and Hudson: New York, 1991, 155–57.

Gadon, Elinor W. *The Once and Future Goddess: A Symbol for Our Time*. New York: Harper and Row, 1989, 245–46; 248.

Kingsley, April. "West Meets East." *Newsweek*, August 20, 1979: 79.

Lippard, Lucy. *Overlay: Contemporary Art and the Art of Prehistory*. London: Pantheon Books, 1983.

Nelson, Mary Carroll. *Connecting: The Art of Beth Ames Swartz*. Flagstaff, AZ: Northland Press, 1984. Introduction by Harry Rand.

Perlman, Barbara. "Arizona: Varied, Energetic and Exciting." *ARTnews*, vol. 79, no. 10 (December 1980): 148–149.

Perreault, John. "Beth Ames Swartz: The Word in Paint." Exh. cat. *The Fire and the Rose*. Vanier Galleries, Scottsdale, AZ and Aspen International Art, Aspen, CO, 2003.

————. "Beth Ames Swartz to the Rescue." *NYArts*, vol. 7, no. 4, (April 2002) 22–3.

————. *Beth Ames Swartz, 1982–1988*. Exh. cat. *A Moving Point of Balance*. Scottsdale, AZ: A Moving Point of Balance, Inc., 1988.

————. *Revelations: The Transformative Impulse in Recent Art*. Exh. cat. Aspen, CO: Aspen Art Museum, 1989.

————. "Impressions of Arizona." *Art in America*, vol. 69, no. 4 (April 1981): 35–45.

"Prints and Photographs Published – Beth Ames Swartz: A Story for the Eleventh Hour." *Print Collector's Newsletter*, vol. 26, no. 3, July–August 1995, 106–107.

Rand, Harry. *Israel Revisited: Beth Ames Swartz*. Exh. cat. Scottsdale, AZ: Beth Ames Swartz, 1981: 40 pp.

————. "Some Notes on the Recent Work of Beth Ames Swartz." *Arts Magazine*, vol. 56 (September 1981): 92–96.

Raven, Arlene. "Beth Ames Swartz: A Story for the Eleventh Hour." *Village Voice*, February 16–March 2, 1994, pp. 88–89.

Reed, Mary Lou. "Beth Ames Swartz's Stylistic Development: 1960–1980," Master's Thesis, Tempe, AZ: Arizona State University, 1981.

Raven, Arlene & Rubin, David S. *Reminders of Invisible Light*. New York: Hudson Hills Press, 2002.

Rothschild, John D. *A Story for the Eleventh Hour*. Exh. cat. New York: E. M. Donahue, 1994. Introduction by Berta Sichel.

_____. *Beth Ames Swartz: The Lotus as Metaphor.* Exh. cat. Scottsdale, AZ: Joy Tash Gallery, 1995.

_____. *Beth Ames Swartz: States of Change.* Essay. Scottsdale, AZ: Vanier Galleries on Marshall Way, 2000.

Seidel, Miriam. "Beth Ames Swartz at E.M. Donahue." *Art in America*, vol. 20, no. 8 (November 1994): 131.

_____. *Beth Ames Swartz: The Shen Qi Series.* Exh. cat. New York, NY: Donahue/Sosinski Art, 1997.

_____. *The Hidden Garden: Three artists explore Kabbalah.* Exh. cat. Philadelphia. PA: The Borowsky Gallery, 2005.

Susser, Deborah Sussman. "National Reviews: Beth Ames Swartz." *ARTnews*, vol. 105, no. 6 (June 2006): 131.

Taylor, Joshua C. *The First Western States Biennial Exhibition.* Exh. cat. Denver: Western States Art Foundation, 1979.

Ten Take Ten. Exh. cat. Colorado Springs: Colorado Springs Fine Arts Center, 1977, 27–9.

Villani, John Carlos. "National Reviews: Beth Ames Swartz." *ARTnews*, vol. 101 no. 51 (May 2002): 75–6.

Visible Reminders. Exh. cat. Scottsdale, AZ. Vanier Galleries, February 7–March 2, 2002.

Wortz, Melinda. Beth Ames Swartz, *Inquiry Into Fire.* Exh. Cat. Scottsdale, AZ: Scottsdale Center for the Arts, 1978, 28 pp.

SELECTED PUBLIC COLLECTIONS
The Brooklyn Museum of Art, Brooklyn, NY
Denver Art Museum, Denver, CO
Everson Museum of Art, Syracuse, NY
Herbert F. Johnson Museum of Art, Cornell University, Ithaca, NY
The Jewish Museum, New York, NY
Joslyn Art Museum, Omaha, NE
National Museum of American Art, Smithsonian Institution, Washington, DC
Phoenix Art Museum, Phoenix, AZ

San Francisco Museum of Modern Art,
San Francisco, CA

Scottsdale Center for the Arts, Museum
of Contemporary Art, Scottsdale, AZ

Skirball Cultural Center, Los Angeles, CA

Skirball Museum, Hebrew Union College,
Cincinnati, OH

Tucson Museum of Art, Tucson, AZ

University Art Museum,
Arizona State University, Tempe, AZ

University of Arizona Museum of Art,
Tucson, AZ

SELECTED HONORS, GRANTS AND OTHER AWARDS

2003   Veteran Feminists of America,
        Medal of Honor, New York, NY

2001   Governor's Arts Award, Phoenix, AZ

2000   Artist in Residence, Anderson
        Ranch, Snowmass Village, CO

1994   Founder, *Culture Care*, an interna-
        tional, non-profit organization
        sponsoring The Sacred Souls
        Project, to identify, support and
        honor individuals who demon-
        strate positive human societal
        values, Phoenix, AZ

1994   Awarded *Flow Fund Grant* by
        Rockefeller Family Fund for
        discretionary philanthropic use
        for non-personal benefit,
        New York, NY

1994   Panelist, College Art Association,
        *Art, Earth and Medicine: A
        Healing Approach*, New York, NY

1993   Panelist, The Sacred in the Arts
        Conference, New York, NY

1992   Speaker, MedArts Conference,
        Research Study on *A Moving
        Point of Balance*, New York, NY

1988   Co-Founder, International
        Friends of Transformative Art
        ("IFTA"), an international, non-
        profit organization for positive
        global change, Phoenix, AZ

1979   Artist in Residence, Volcano Art
        Center, Hawaii National Park, HI

1958–60 New York University,
         Master of Arts

1953–57 Cornell University,
         Bachelor of Science

DONALD KUSPIT

Donald Kuspit is one of America's most distinguished art critics. Winner of the prestigeous Frank Jewett Mather Award for Distinction in Art Criticism (1983), given by the College Art Association. Professor Kuspit is a Contributing Editor at *Artforum, Sculpture,* and *Tema Celeste* magazines, the Editor of *Art Criticism,* and on the advisory board of *Centennial Review.*

He has doctorates in philosophy (University of Frankfurt) and art history (University of Michigan), as well as degrees from Columbia University, Yale University, and Pennsylvania State University.

He has also completed the course of study at the Psychoanalytic Institute of the New York University Medical Center.

He received honorary doctorates in fine arts from Davidson College (1993) and the San Francisco Institute of Art (1996). In 1997 the National Association of the Schools of Art and Design gave him a Citation for Distinguished Service to the Visual Arts. In 1998 he received an honorary doctorate of humane letters from the University of Illinois at Urbana-Champaign. In 2000 he delivered the Getty Lectures at the University of Southern California.

He is Professor of Art History and Philosophy at the State University of New York at Stony Brook, and has been the A. D. White Professor-at-Large at Cornell University (1991–97). He has received fellowships from the Ford Foundation, Fulbright Commission, National Endowment for the Humanities, National Endowment for the Arts, Guggenheim Foundation, and Asian Cultural Council, among other organizations. He has written numerous articles, exhibition reviews, and catalogue essays, and lectured at many universities and art schools.

He is the editorial advisor for European art 1900-50 and art criticism for the new

Encyclopedia Britannica (16th edition), and wrote the entry on Art Criticism for it. He is on the advisory board of the Lucy Daniels Foundation for the psychoanalytic study of creativity. His most recent books are *The Cult of the Avant-Garde Artist* (New York: Cambridge University Press, 1993; also in German, Klagenfurt: Ritter Verlag, 1995), *The Dialectic of Decadence* (New York: Stux Press, 1993; reissued New York: Allworth Press, 2000), *The New Subjectivism: Art in the 1980s* (Ann Arbor: UMI Research Press, 1988; reissued New York: Da Capo Press, 1993), *The Photography of Albert Renger-Patzsch* (New York: Aperture, 1993), *Signs of Psyche in Modern and Postmodern Art* (New York: Cambridge University Press, 1994; also in Spanish, Madrid: Akal, 2002), *Primordial Presences: The Sculpture of Karel Appel* (New York: Abrams, 1994), *Health and Happiness in Twentieth Century Avant-Garde Art* (Ithaca: Cornell University Press, 1996), *Idiosyncratic Identities: Artists at the End of the Avant-Garde* (New York: Cambridge University Press, 1996), *Chihuly* (New York: Abrams, 1997), *Jamali* (New York: Rizzoli, 1997; reissue with expanded text, 2004), *Joseph Raffael* (New York: Abbeville, 1998), *Daniel Brush* (New York: Abrams, 1998), *Hans Hartung* (Antibes/Nagoya: Aichi Museum of Art, 1998), *The Rebirth of Painting in the Late 20th Century* (New York: Cambridge University Press, 2000), *Psychostrategies of Avant Garde Art* (New York: Cambridge University Press, 2000), *Redeeming Art: Critical Reveries* (New York: Allworth Press, 2000), *Don Eddy* (New York: Hudson Hills, 2002), *Hunt Slonem* (New York: Abrams, 2002), *Hans Breder* (Münster: Hackmeister, 2002), *Steven Tobin* (New York: Hudson Hills, 2003), *April Gornik* (New York: Hudson Hills, 2004), and *The End of Art* (New York: Cambridge University Press, 2004). He has also written *Clement Greenberg, Art Critic*; *Leon Golub: Existentialist/Activist Painter*; *Eric Fischl*; *Louise Bourgeois*; *Alex Katz: Night Paintings*; and *The Critic Is Artist: The Intentionality of Art*.

JOHN D. ROTHSCHILD

John D. Rothschild holds a M.B.A from Columbia University and a B.S from Massachusetts Institute of Technology. He has worked as an art dealer for over thirty years serving as President of Rothschild Fine Arts, Inc. in New York and Arizona as well as serving as President, Vanier Galleries, Scottsdale, AZ. He is the author works on the art of Joel Coplin, Duffy Sheridan and Beth Ames Swartz as well as a published poet.

Works in English on Poetry of Du Fu and Li Bai

BIBLIOGRAPHY COMPILED BY JOHN D. ROTHSCHILD

Alley, Rewi, trans. *Du Fu: Selected Poems*. Beijing: Foreign Language Press, 1962 (as *Tu Fu: Selected Poems*), 2001. [ISBN–10: 7119028898 (paperback)] Part of a multivolume work: Hong Shen, et al. *The Cream of Classical Chinese Literature, Vol. 2*. Beijing: Foreign Language Press, 2001. [ISBN–10: 7119025236 / ISBN–13: 9787119025230]

Ayscough, Florence Wheelock and Lowell, Amy, trans. *Fir-Flower Tablets: Poems Translated from the Chinese*. Boston: Houghton Mifflin, 1921, Reprinted, February 1926. Online: http://digital.library.upenn.edu/women/lowell/tablets/tablets.html#115; PDF: http://www.archive.org/details/firflowertablets00ayscuoft
_____. *The Autobiography of a Chinese Poet, Vol. I, A.D. 712–759*. Boston: HoughtonMifflin, 1929.
_____. *Travels of a Chinese Poet: Tu Fu, Guest of Rivers and Lakes, Vol. II, A.D. 759–770*. Boston: Houghton Mifflin, 1934.

Barnstone Tony and Chou, Ping, ed. & trans. *The Anchor Book of Chinese Poetry*. New York: Random House, Inc., 2005. [ISBN–10: 0385721986 / ISBN–13: 9780385721981]

Birch, Cyril, ed. *Anthology of Chinese Literature, Volume 1: From Early Times to the Fourteenth Century*. Random House, 1965, 1972; New York: Grove Press, 1965, 1987, 1994. [ISBN–10: 0394177665 / ISBN–13: 9780394177663 (1965, hardback); ISBN–10: 0394476425 / ISBN–13: 978–0394476421 (1972, hardback); ISBN–10: 0802150381 / ISBN–13: 978–0802150387 (1994, paperback)]

Bynner, Witter and Kiang Kang-hu, trans. *The Jade Mountain: a Chinese Anthology, Being Three Hundred Poems of the T'ang Dynasty: 618–906*. New York: Alfred A Knopf, 1929; 4th e, 1931, renewed copyright 1957; New York: Vintage Books, 1972. [ISBN–10: 0394718410 / ISBN–13: 9780394718415 (paperback)] Online: http://etext.lib.virginia.edu/chinese/frame.htm; http://afpc.asso.fr/wengu/wg/wengu.php?l=Tangshi&no=-1 ; http://zhongwen.com/tangshi.htm

Chou, Eva Shan. *Reconsidering Tu Fu: Literary Greatness and Cultural Context*. Cambridge: Cambridge University Press, 1995, 1998 transferred to digital. [ISBN–10: 0521440394 / ISBN–13: 9780521440394 (hardback); ISBN–10: 0521028280 / ISBN–13: 9780521028288 (2006, paperback)]

Cooper, Arthur R. V. *Li Po and Tu Fu*. London, Penguin Books, 1973, 1986, 2006. [ISBN-10: 0140442723 / ISBN-13: 9780140442724 (paperback)]

Cranmer-Byng, L. (Launcelot). *A Lute of Jade: Being Selections from the Classical Poets of China*. New York: E. P. Dutton and Company, 1918. Online: http://www.archive.org/details/aluteofjadeselec00390gu

Davis, A(lbert) R(ichard). *Tu Fu*. New York: Twayne Publishers, 1971. [ISBN-10: 0805728988 / ISBN-13: 978-0805728989 (hardback)]

Eide, Elling O., trans. *Poems by Li Po*. Lexington, KY: Anvil Press, 1983 (150 copies). _____. *On Li Po*; in Wright, Arthur F. & Twitchett, Denis, eds. *Perspectives on the T'ang*. New Haven: Yale University Press, 1973. [ISBN-10: 0300015224 / ISBN-13: 9780300015225 (hardback); ISBN-10: 0300026749 / ISBN-13: 9780300026740 (1981, paperback)]

Fletcher, W. J. B. *Gems of Chinese Verse*. Shanghai: Commercial Press Limited, 1919. Online: http://www.archive.org/details/gemsofchineseveroofletiala _____. *More Gems of Chinese Poetry*. Shanghai: Commercial Press Limited, 1919. Online: http://ebook.lib.hku.hk/CADAL/B31396227/

Fung, Sydney S.K. & Lai, S. T. *25 Tang Poets: Index to the English Translations*. New York: Columbia University Press, 1984. [ISBN-10: 9622012973 / ISBN-13: 9789622012974 (hardback)]

Giles, Herbert A., ed. *Gems of Chinese Literature, Prose and Verse, Vol. II (Verse)*. London: Bernard Quaritch, 1884. Shanghai: Kelly & Walsh, Ltd. 1923. 2nd ed. Online PDF: http://books.google.com/books?hl=en&id=NhkiAAAAMAAJ&dq=giles+1884+chinese+herbert&printsec=frontcover&source=web&ots=lVqlLTIQNZ&sig=qFBoFupAFBFRIxARP8AqqEfsMa8 _____. *Chinese Poetry in English Verse*. London: Bernard Quaritch; Shanghai: Kelly & Walsh, 1898. _____. *History of Chinese Literature*. New York: D Appleton-Century Co., 1901, 1915, 1923, 1933. (hardback) [ISBN-10: 111739977X / ISBN-13: 9781117399775 (paperback)] New York: Grove Press, 1923, 1958 (hardback). New York: Frederick Ungar Publishing, 1967 (hardback). Rutland VT & Tokyo: Tuttle Publishing, 1973. [ISBN-10: 127 / ISBN-13: 978-0804810975 (paperback)] Kessinger Publishing, 2007. [ISBN-10: 1432517163 / ISBN-13: 978-1432517168 (paperback)]

Giles, Herbert A. & Waley, Arthur, trans. *Selected Chinese Verses*. Shanghai: Commercial Press Limited, 1934.

Graham, A. C., trans. *Poems of the Late T'ang*. Harmondsworth, Middlesex, England: Penguin Books, 1965, 1977. [ISBN–10: 0140441573 / ISBN–13: 978–0140441574 (softcover)]; New York: New York Review Books, 2008, 19. [ISBN–10: 1590172574 ISBN–13: 9781590172575 (paperback)]

Hamill, Sam, trans. *Facing the Snow: Visions of Tu Fu*. Buffalo, NY: White Pine Press, 1988. [ISBN–10: 0934834245 / ISBN–13: 978–0934834247 (paperback)]
_____. *Endless River: Li Po and Tu Fu*, a Friendship in Poetry. New York: Weatherhill, 1993. [ISBN–10: 0834802635 / ISBN–13: 9780834802636 (paperback)]
_____. *Midnight Flute: Chinese Poems of Love and Longing*. New York: Shambhala, 1994. [ISBN–10: 0877739137 / ISBN–13: 978–0877739135 (paperback)]
_____. *Crossing the Yellow River: 300 Poems from the Chinese*. Rochester, NY: BOA Editions, 2000. [ISBN–10: 1880238977 / ISBN–13: 978–1880238974 (hardback); [ISBN–10: 1880238985 / ISBN–13: 978–1880238981 (paperback)]

Hamill, Sam and Seaton, J.P., eds. and trans. *The Poetry of Zen*. Boston & London: Shambhala, 2004. [ISBN–10: 1570628637 / ISBN–13: 978–1570628634 (hardback); ISBN–10: 159030425X / ISBN–13: 978–1590304259 (2007, paperback)]

Hart, Henry Hersch, comp. & trans. *The Hundred Names: A Short Introduction to the Study of Chinese Poetry with Illustrative Translations*. Berkeley, CA: University of California Press, 1933, reprinted 1938, Stanford University [2nd ed.],1954; Greenwood Press; [3rd ed.],1968, reprinted 1972, 128.
_____. *The Charcoal Burner, and Other Poems; Original Translations from the Poetry of the Chinese*. Norman: University of Oklahoma Press, 1974. [ISBN–10: 0806111852 / ISBN–13: 9780806111858 (hardback); ISBN–10: 0806114754 / ISBN13: 9780806114750 (paperback)]

Hawkes, David. *A Little Primer on Tu Fu*. Oxford: Oxford University Press, 1967; Boston: Cheng & Tsui Co., 1988. [ISBN–10: 0198154305 / ISBN–13: 978–0198154303 (hardback); ISBN–10: 9627255025 Y ISBN–13: 978–9627255024 (paperback)]

Herdan, Innes, trans. & Yee, Chiang, illus. *300 T'ang Poems*. Taipei: Far East Book Company, 1973 (hardback), 1979 1984 (4th ed. hardback), 2000 (paperback), 2005 (paperback). [ISBN–10: 9576124719 / ISBN–13: 978–9576124716]

Hinton, David, trans. *The Selected Poems of Tu Fu*. New York, New Directions Publishing Corporation, 1988, 1989. [ISBN–10: 0811210995 / ISBN–13: 978–0811210997 (hardback); ISBN: 0811211002 / ISBN–13: 978–0811211000 (paperback)]

_____. *The Selected Poems of Li Po*. New York, New Directions Publishing Corporation, 1996. [ISBN–10: 0811213234 / ISBN–13: 978–0811213233 (paperback)]; Lexington, KY: Anvil Press, 1998. [ISBN–10: 0856462918 / ISBN–13: 978–0856462917 (paperback)]

Holyoak, Keith, trans. *Facing the Moon: Poems of Li Bai and Du Fu*. Durham, NH: Oyster River, 2007. [ISBN–10: 1882291042 / ISBN–13: 9781882291045]

Hung, William. *A Concordance to the Poetry of Tu Fu*. Harvard-Yenching Institute Sinological Index Series, Supplement 14, 3 vols. Peiping: Harvard-Yenching, 1940.

_____. *Tu Fu: China's Greatest Poet*. Cambridge, Harvard University Press, 1952. [ISBN: 0758143222 (hardback)]

_____. *Supplementary Volume of Notes for "Tu Fu: China's Greatest Poet"* Cambridge, Harvard University Press, 1952. [ISBN–10: 0674856058 / ISBN–13: 9780674856059 (hardback)]

Jenyns, Soame. *Selections from the Three Hundred Poems of the T'ang Dynasty*, London: John Murray, 1940.

Johnson, Stephen M. *Fifty Tang Poems*. San Francisco: Pocketscholar Press, 2000. [ISBN–10: 0967945305 / ISBN–13: 978–0967945309 (paperback)]

Kizer, Carolyn Ashley. *Knock Upon Silence*. Garden City NY: Doubleday, 1965. Seattle: University of Washington Press, 1968. [ISBN 10: 0385045808 / ISBN 13: 9780385045803 (hardback); ISBN–10: 0295738456 / ISBN–13: 9780295738451 (paperback)]

_____. *Carrying Over: Poems from the Chinese, Urdu, Macedonian, Yiddish, and French African*. Port Townsend, WA: Copper Canyon Press, 1988, 1989. [ISBN 10: 1556590172 / ISBN–13: 9781556590177 (paperback, 1988); ISBN–10: 1556590164 / ISBN–13: 978–1556590160 (hardback, 1989)]

Kline, A. S. *Like Water or Clouds: The T'ang Dynasty and the Tao*. Online: http://www.tonykline.co.uk/PITBR/Chinese/Allwaterhome.htm.

Li Weijian, trans., Weng Xianliang, reviser. *Selected Poems of Du Fu*. Chengdu: Sichuan People's Publishing House, 1981, 1985.

Liu, James J. Y. *The Art of Chinese Poetry*. Chicago: University of Chicago Press, 1962.
[ISBN–10: 0226486869 (hardback) / ISBN–10: 022648687–7 (paperback)]

Liu, Wu-chi and Lo, Irving Yucheng, eds. *Sunflower Splendor: Three Thousand Years of Chinese Poetry*. Bloomington: Indiana University Press, 1975, 1990. [ISBN–10: 025335580X / ISBN–13: 978–0253355805 (hardback); ISBN–10: 0253206073 / ISBN–13: 978–0253206077 (1990, paperback)]

Man, Wong, trans. *Poems from the Chinese*. Hong Kong: Creation Books, 1950.

Mc Craw, David R. *Du Fu's Laments from the South*. Honolulu: University of Hawaii Press, 1992.
[ISBN–10: 082481455X / ISBN–13: 978–0824814557 (paperback)]

Minford, John and Lau, Joseph S. M., eds. *Classical Chinese Literature*. New York: Columbia University Press, 2000; reprint 2002. [ISBN–10: 0231096763 / ISBN–13: 978–0231096768 (2000, hardback); ISBN–10: 0231096771 / ISBN–13: 978–0231096775 (2002, paperback)]. Hong Kong, The Chinese University Press, 2000. [ISBN–10: 9622016251 (hardback); ISBN–10: 9629960486 (paperback)]

Neinhauser, William H., Jr., Hartman, C., Ma, Y. W., & West, Stephen H. *Indiana Companion to Traditional Chinese Literature, Vol. 1*. Bloomington-Indianapolis: Indiana University Press, 1986.

Neinhauser, William H., Jr., Hartman, Charles & Galer, Scott. W., eds.. *The Indiana Companion to Traditional Chinese Literature, Vol. 2*. Bloomington-Indianapolis: Indiana University Press, 1998.
[ISBN–10: 025333456X / ISBN–13: 978–0253334565 (hardback)]

Obata, Shigeyoshi, trans. *The Works of Li Po, The Chinese Poet*. New York: E. P. Dutton & Co., 1922.
(see: http://ebook.lib.hku.hk/CADAL/B31400723/index.html) Whitefish, MT: Kessinger Publishing, 2007.
[ISBN–10: 054876591X / ISBN–13: 978–0548765913]

Owen, Stephen. *The Poetry of the Early T'ang*. New Haven: Yale University Press, 1977.
[ISBN–10: 0300021038 / ISBN–13: 9780300021035 (hardback)]
_____. *The Great Age of Chinese Poetry: The High T'ang*. New Haven: Yale University Press, 1980.
[ISBN–10: 0300023677 / ISBN–13: 9780300023671 (hardback)]
_____. *The Late Tang: Chinese Poetry of the Mid-Ninth Century*. Cambridge: Harvard University Press, 2007.
[ISBN–10: 0674021371 / ISBN–13: 9780674021372]

_____. *An Anthology of Chinese Literature: Beginnings to 1911.* New York: W.W. Norton and Co., 1996.
[ISBN-10: 0393038238 / ISBN-13: 978-0393038231 (hardback);
ISBN-10: 0393971066 / ISBN-13: 978-0393971064 (1997, paperback)]

Payne, Robert, ed. *The White Pony: an Anthology of Chinese Poetry.* New York: John Day Company, 1947.
[ASIN: B000WSLOLE / ISBN-10 1399645943 / ISBN-13 9781399645942 (hardback). London:
G.Allen & Unwin, 1949 [ASIN: B0007ILS24 (hardback)] New York: Mentor (The New American
Library of World Literature), 1960. [ISBN-10: 045161111X / ISBN-13: 978-0451611116 (paperback)]

Pine, Red (aka Porter, Bill). *Poems of the Masters: China's Classic Anthology of T'ang and Sung Dynasty Verse.*
Port Townsend WA: Copper Canyon Press, 2003.
[ISBN-10: 1556591950 / ISBN-13: 978-1556591952 (paperback)]

Pound, Ezra, trans. *Cathay . . . For The Most Part From The Chinese Of Rihaku, From The Notes Of The Late Ernest Fenollosa,
And The Decipherings Of The Professors Mori And Ariga.* London: Elkin Mathews, 1915. Online:
http://paintedricecakes.org/languagearts/poetry/cathay_pound.html

Rexroth, Kenneth. *One Hundred Poems from the Chinese.* New York, New Directions Publishing Corporation, 1971.
[ISBN-10: 0811201805 (paperback)]

Seaton, J. P. & Cryer, James, trans. *Bright Moon, Perching Birds: Poems.* Middletown, CT: Wesleyan University Press,
1971, 1987. [ISBN-10: 0819521434 / ISBN-13: 9780819521439 (hardback); ISBN-10: 0819511447
/ ISBN-13: 978-0819511447 (paperback)]

Seaton, J. P. & Maloney, Dennis, eds. *A Drifting Boat: An Anthology of Chinese Zen Poetry.* Fredonia, NY: White Pine
Press, 1994. [ISBN-10: 1877727377 / ISBN-13: 9781877727375 (paperback)]

Seaton, J.P. *The Shambhala Anthology of Chinese Poetry.* Boulder: Shambhala, 2006.
[ISBN-10: 1570628629 / ISBN-13: 978-1570628627 (paperback)]

Seth, Vikram, trans. *Three Chinese Poets: Translations of Poems by Wang Wei, Li Bai, and Du Fu.* London: Faber & Faber,
1992. [ISBN-10: 0571166539 / ISBN-13: 978-0571166534 (hardback)] New York: HarperPerennial, 1992.
[ISBN-10: 0060553529 / ISBN-13: 978-0060553524 (hardback); ISBN-10: 0060950242 / ISBN-13:
978-0060950248 (1993, paperback)] London: Phoenix (an Imprint of The Orion Publishing Group Ltd),
1997 [ISBN-10: 1857997808 / ISBN-13: 978-1857997804 (paperback)]

Stimson, Hugh M. *Fifty-Five T'ang Poems: A Text in the Reading and Understanding of T'ang Poetry (Far Eastern Publications Series)*. New Haven: Yale University Press, 1976. [ISBN–10: 0887100260 / ISBN–13: 978–0887100260 (paperback)]

Turner, John, trans. & Deeney, John J., ed. *Golden Treasury of Chinese Poetry*. Seattle: University of Washington Press, 1976. [ISBN–10: 0295955066 / ISBN–13: 978–0295955063 (hardback)]; Berkeley, CA: Small Press Distribution; 1989 revsd. [ISBN–10: 9627255041 / ISBN–13: 978–9627255048 (paperback)]

Underwood, Edna Worthley & Chu, Chi Hwang. *Tu Fu: Wanderer and Minstrel Under Moons of Cathay*. Portland, ME: Mosher Press, 1929.

Varsano, Paula M. *Li Bo, Tracking the Banished Immortal, The Poetry of Li Bo and Its Critical Reception*. Honolulu: University of Hawaii Press, 2003. [ISBN–10: 0828482573X / ISBN–13: 978–0824825737 (hardback)]

Waley, Arthur D. *A Hundred and Seventy Chinese Poems, Vol. I; More Translations from the Chinese, Vol. II*. New York: Alfred A Knopf, 1919. (Online: http://www.gutenberg.org/files/16500/16500.txt) Sandwich: Chapman Billies, 1997. [ISBN–10: 0939218178]
_____. *The Poetry and Career of Li Po*. New York: Macmillan Co., 1950; London: George Allen & Unwin, 1950, 2nd ed., 1958; 3rd ed., 1969, 4th ed, 1979. [ISBN–10: 0048950122 (hardback)]

Watson, Burton, ed. & trans. *The Columbia Book of Chinese Poetry: From Early Times to the Thirteenth Century*. New York: Columbia University Press, 1984. [ISBN–10: 0231056826 / ISBN–13: 978–0231056823 (hardback); ISBN–10: 0231056834 / ISBN–13: 978–0231056830 (paperback)]
_____. *The Selected Poems of Du Fu*. New York: Columbia University Press, 2002. [ISBN–10: 0231128290 (paperback) / ISBN–13: 9780231128292 (hardback)]

Weinberger, Eliot, ed. *The New Directions Anthology of Classical Chinese Poetry. New York: New Directions Publishing Corporation, 2003, 2004*. [ISBN–10: 0811215407 / ISBN–13: 978–0811215404 (2003, hardback); ISBN–10: 0811216055 / ISBN–13: 978–0811216050 (2004, paperback)]

Williams, An-li Chang. *Li Bo: Poet Immortal*. London: Serendipity, 2003. [ISBN–10: 1843940426 / ISBN–13: 978–1843940425]
_____. *More Li Bo Poems: Supplementary to Biography Li Bo –Poet Immortal*. Victoria, Canada: Trafford On Demand

Publishing, [ISBN–10: 1412026768 / ISBN–13: 978–1412026765 (paperback)]

Whincup, Greg. *The Heart of Chinese Poetry*. Garden City: Anchor Press, Doubleday, 1987. [ISBN–10: 038523967X / ISBN 978–0385239677]

Wu, Juntao, trans. *Tu Fu–a New Translation*. Hong Kong: The Commercial Press Ltd, 1981. [ISBN–10: 9620710126 / ISBN13: 9789620710124 (hardback)]

Yang, Hsein, Yang, Xianyi, trans. & Gladys, trans. *Poetry and Prose of the T'ang and Song*. Beijing: China Books & Periodicals (Panda Books), 1984. [ISBN–10: 0835111644 / ISBN–13: 9780835111645 (paperback)]

Yip, Wai-Lim, ed. & trans.. *Chinese Poetry: Major Modes and Genres*. Berkeley: University of California Press, 1976, Durham: Duke University Press, 1997 (2nd rev.). [ISBN–10: 0822319519 / ISBN–13: 978–0822319511 (1997 hardback); ISBN–10: 0822319462 / ISBN–13: 978–0822319467 (1997 paperback)]

Young, David. *Five T'ang Poets*. Oberlin: Oberlin College Press, 1990.

HELPFUL INTERNET SITES

300 Tang Poems:	http://afpc.asso.fr/wengu/wg/wengu.php?l=Tangshi&no=-1
	http://etext.lib.virginia.edu/chinese/frame.htm
	http://zhongwen.com/tangshi.htm
T'ang Poetry:	http://www.chinapage.com/poetry9.html
	http://www.chinese-poems.com/
Dictionary:	http://www.chinalanguage.com/dictionaries/ccdict/
	http://www.mandarintools.com/

Acknowledgements

Many people contributed their enthusiasm and their hard work toward making *The Word in Paint* possible.

We would like to express our appreciation to Tom Cooper and to personnel at Arizona State University including Jewell Parker Rhodes, Elizabeth Apodaca, Matthew R. Brennan, Haiying Dong, Debra Friedman, Mengying Li, Scott P. Muir and other faculty and staff of the Virginia G Piper Center for Creative Writing as well as those at the College of Public Programs at the ASU Downtown Phoenix Campus.

We acknowledge the contribution of art critic John Perreault who first applied the phrase, The Word in Paint, to the work of Beth Ames Swartz.

We also would like to thank owners of works of art reproduced herein for their continuing support:

Susan & Eliot Black, Greenwich, CT
Doris & Brooks DuBose, Paradise Valley, AZ
Sarah Dutton, New York, NY
Ursula & Stephan Gebert, Paradise Valley, AZ
Mary & Douglas Jorden, Scottsdale, AZ
Eric Jungermann, Phoenix, AZ
Sharon Orth Lewis & Delbert Lewis, Phoenix, AZ
Sylvia Levin, Santa Monica, CA
Peri Nielsen, Portola Valley, CA
Phoenix Art Museum, Phoenix, AZ
Ann B. Ritt, Haverford PA
Laura & Herb Roskind, Oak Bluffs, MA
Marcia & Sanford Roth, Paradise Valley, AZ
Jada Pinkett Smith & Will Smith, Calabasas, CA
Diane & Gary Tooker, Scottsdale, AZ
Beth Ames Swartz, Paradise Valley, AZ

GRATEFUL ACKNOWLEDGEMENT is made to the following translators into English (and their publishers) who own the copyright to these translations of the individual poems by Du Fu and Li Bai.

Barnstone Tony: "Facing Snow" [132-3] by Du Fu, translated by Tony Barnstone, from *The Anchor Book of Chinese Poetry*, copyright ©2005 by Tony Barnstone and Chou, Ping, ed. Reprinted by permission of Tony Barnstone.

BOA Editions, Ltd.: "Zazen on Ching-t'ing Mountain" [94] by Li Bai, and "Evening near Serpent River" [111] and "Departing from Ch'in-chou" [143-4] by Du Fu, translated by Sam Hamill, from *Crossing the Yellow River: 300 Poems from the Chinese*, copyright ©2000. Reprinted by permission of BOA Editions, Ltd.

Harvard University Press: "The Mei-Pei Lake" [53-4, XIX]; "Sleepless Night" [214, CCLVII] and "Overnight in the Apartment by the River [231, CCLXXVII] all by Tu Fu (Du Fu) translated by William Hung, from *Tu Fu: China's Greatest Poet*, copyright ©1952. Reprinted by permission of Harvard University Press.

David Hinton. "Standing Alone" [26, 161] by Tu Fu (Du Fu), translated by David Hinton, from *The Selected Poems of Tu Fu*, copyright ©1988, ©1989; "Facing Snow" [46] by Tu Fu (Du Fu), translated by David Hinton, from *The Selected Poems of Tu Fu*, copyright ©1988, ©1989; and "After an Ancient Poem" [110] by Li Po (Li Bai), translated by David Hinton, from *The Selected Poems of Li Po* copyright ©1996. Reprinted by permission of David Hinton.

Keith Holyoak: "Facing Snow" [102-3] by Du Fu, from *Facing the Moon: Poems of Li Bai and Du Fu*, copyright ©2007. Reprinted by permission of Keith Holyoak.

Carolyn Ashley Kizer: "Too Much Heat, Too Much Work" [29] by Du Fu, from *Carrying Over: Poems from the Chinese Urdu Macedonian Yiddish and French African*, copyright ©1988. Reprinted by permission of Carolyn Ashley Kizer.

New Directions Publishing Corporation: "Night in the House by the River" [XXX, 29] by Du Fu, translated by Kenneth Rexroth, from *One Hundred Poems from the Chinese*, copyright ©1971. Reprinted by permission of New Directions Publishing Corp.

Random House, Inc.: "Endless Yearning I" by Li Bai; "A Night Abroad" and "A View of the Wilderness" by Du Fu, translated by Witter Bynner, from *Jade Mountain: A Chinese Anthology (Being 300 Poems of the T'ang Dynasty (618-906)*, copyright ©1929, renewal copyright ©1957. Reprinted by permission of Random House, Inc.

University of California Press: "War" [128] by Du Fu, translated by Henry Hersch Hart, from *The Hundred Names: A Short Introduction to the Study of Chinese Poetry with Illustrative Translations*. copyright ©1933, reprinted 1938, Stanford University Press, 2nd ed., 1954; Greenwood Press; 3rd ed., 1968, reprinted 1972. Reprinted by permission of University of California Press.

Yale University Press: "Facing the Snow" [201, 390-1] by Du Fu, translated by Stephen Owen, from *The Great Age of Chinese Poetry: the High T'ang*, copyright ©1981. Reprinted by permission of Yale University Press.